CHINA,

COVID-19,

WORLD DOMINATION

By Dr. Alan Pateman

By Dr. Jennifer Pateman

Available from APMI Publications, Amazon.com and Other Retail Outlets

It's almost straight out of a movie – let's cause the world to get a virus and let's profit off of it.

-- *Jeremy Alters*

Chief Strategist Berman Law Group,
Miami, Florida, USA

CHINA, COVID-19, WORLD DOMINATION

DR. ALAN PATEMAN

❖

Book 2 of a 4 Book Series

BOOK TITLE:
China, Covid-19, World Domination

WRITTEN BY Dr. ALAN PATEMAN
ISBN: 978-1-909132-85-6
eBook ISBN: 978-1-909132-86-3

Published By:
APMI Publications
In Partnership with Truth for the Journey Books **36**
Email: publications@alanpateman.com
www.AlanPatemanMinistries.com

Acknowledgements:
Author/Design/Senior Editor/Publisher: Apostle Dr. Alan Pateman
Editing/Proofreading/Research: Dr. Jennifer Pateman
Computer Administration/Office Manager: Dr. Dorothea Struhlik
Cover Image Credit: www.PosterMyWall.com

Unless otherwise indicated, all scriptural quotations are from the HOLY BIBLE, NEW INTERNATIONAL VERSION ®. NIV ®. Copyright © 1973, 1978, 1984 by the International Bible Society. Used by permission of Zondervan Publishing House. All rights reserved.

*Where scriptures appear with special emphasis (**in bold**, italic or <u>underlined</u>) we have edited them ourselves in order to bring focused attention within the context of this subject being taught.*

❖

Table of Contents

❖

Acknowledgement

I just want to thank the Lord for his direction in writing this book; I also want to thank the Holy Spirit for his direction in *decoding* what's going on in the world, showing us how to *interpret these times* we live in.

Also to thank my wife Jenny, for her writing and research skills, it must be said that I would not be able to bring this book to life without her partnership and specific skill-set. She is able to catch and de-code what is in my spirit. God has truly made us *"one"* in order to flow together in this way and bring books of prophetic insight to you. Helping others de-crypt what's happening in the nations in this moment.

It's all about NATIONS AND KINGDOMS:

*To the one who is victorious and does my will to the end, I will give authority over the **nations**...*

(Revelation 2:26)

*Then I was told, "You must prophesy again about many peoples, **nations**, languages and **kings**."*

(Revelation 10:11)

*On each side of the river stood the tree of life, bearing twelve crops of fruit, yielding its fruit every month. **And the leaves** [we are the leaves] **of the tree are for the healing of the nations.***

(Revelation 22:2 – bracket added)

*See, I have appointed you this day over the **nations and over the kingdoms,** to uproot and break down, to destroy and to overthrow, to build and to plant.*

(Jeremiah 1:10 AMP)

*And to Him (the Messiah) was given dominion (supreme authority), Glory and a **kingdom,** that all the peoples, nations, and speakers of every language should serve and worship Him. His dominion is an everlasting dominion, which will not pass away; and **His kingdom is one, which will not be destroyed.***

(Daniel 7:14 AMP)

*In the days of those [final ten] kings the God of heaven will set up a **kingdom** that will never be destroyed...*

(Daniel 2:44 AMP)

Acknowledgement

*His kingdom is an everlasting **kingdom** and His dominion is from generation to generation.*
                                        (Daniel 4:3 AMP)

*These four great beasts are four kings who will arise from the earth. But the saints (believers) of the Most High [God] **will receive the kingdom and possess the kingdom** forever, for all ages to come... and the time arrived when **the saints (believers) took possession of the kingdom.** Then the kingdom and the dominion and the greatness of all the kingdoms under the whole heaven will be given to the people of the saints (believers) of the Most High; **His kingdom will be an everlasting kingdom,** and all the dominions will serve and obey Him.*
                                        (Daniel 7:17-18, 21-22, 27 AMP)

❖

Introduction

S ome may ask me, "Why are you writing a book all about China, Covid-19, World Domination?" To answer this I must start by saying, Jesus Himself told us to go into *"all the world,"* and this includes China.

Traveling there and taking photos for Instagram, *(just so that we can say that we went),* is not enough, although that's great. But we need to go with our prayers and intellect, not just our feet, luggage, hotel reservations, airfare and passports.

Prayers supersede all this, because there is no distance in the spirit. A lot of ground can be covered, especially through prophetic intercession.

It's also true to say, in reaching *"all the world"* we can use all methods available, including technology. Jesus never said we should vote with our feet, only. The Divine Commission isn't self-absorbing and deluded. It causes us to be mindful of the Nations. Not oblivious or indifferent. Most people live in a state of denial, escapism or even nihilism, but none of this is Christianity. Trivializing or turning a blind eye to what God's orchestrating in the nations is folly. Ignorance is not bliss. Ignorant people always get hurt.

During the culmination of this age, much is unfolding and CHINA is a big player in this. Our limited ideas and religious impressions cannot be what lead us. We must seek God's mind and not set our own course. We must be on the same page as God, otherwise we will end up fighting Him and getting in His way. We must know His heart, His timing and agenda, because *"set times,"* declared throughout scripture, cannot be deviated from.

The Great Commission

Then the eleven disciples went to Galilee, to the mountain where Jesus had told them to go. When they saw him, they worshiped him; but some doubted. Then Jesus came to them and said, **"All authority in heaven and on earth has been given to me. Therefore go and make disciples of all nations,** *baptizing them in the name of the Father and of the Son and of the Holy Spirit, and teaching them to obey everything I have commanded you. And surely I am with you always, to the very end of the age."*

(Matthew 28:16-20)

16

*He said to them, **"Go into all the world** and preach the gospel to all creation. Whoever believes and is baptized will be saved, but whoever does not believe will be condemned. And these signs will accompany those who believe: In my name they will drive out demons; they will speak in new tongues; they will pick up snakes with their hands; and when they drink deadly poison, it will not hurt them at all; they will place their hands on sick people, and they will get well."*

(Mark 16:15-18)

It has to be said, that many Christians are not interested in world events at all. They prickle somewhat and get indignant if a preacher gets remotely political! They bore easily. THEN they wonder why their local governments won't help them.

This must change if we desire to see a global impact through and by the body of Christ.

❖

CHAPTER 1

China's Ambitions & Cover Up

China wants to be TOP of the Food Chain!

As we begin this book *(which is book 2 in a 4 book series)* it is important to mention China's aspirations to be a world ruler, and with good reason. For China does not want to be part of some elite ruling class. No. It wants to be THE WORLD RULER *(under a whole new world order)*. And according to some experts, China is not willing to share this poll position.

Something to do with an ancient Chinese myth, concerning an Emperor who ordered every other sun to be removed from the sky because there was only room for ONE! *(I did find this particular myth online or some variation of it and the sentiments are clear. REMOVE THE COMPETITION!)*[1]

They *(China)* are actively buying up the world. Vacuuming up assets from all over the world and have been engaged in this for decades. They are everywhere including Africa. They are buying up landmass and trade roots to exact their long-term goals and strategic plans. Going forwards as you read this book, you will notice that EVERYTHING about China has been and still is LONG TERM.

They are patient, relentless and very thorough. Let me be specific: It's the CCP Chinese Communist Party that are ruthless. The hard working people of China are another story. And many of them no longer trust their own government and there is a great desire for change.

Wuhan Locals don't Trust their own Government

Jenny my wife has friends at our daughter's school who lived close to Wuhan and had friends in the same area. These friends escaped, to Italy, *(where they plan to stay for one year, because it's not safe to go back)*. However, in discussion with my wife, she was told that no one trusts the government there. And although they can't be open about it, still the general feeling is thus regardless. Everyone stays quiet, but the prevailing sentiment is an open secret nonetheless.

It was further described to my wife, how once those new hospitals went up and were built so quickly, the local people of Wuhan were even more suspicious. Officials immediately began dragging infected people from their homes *(all those in quarantine and voluntary self isolation)*. They were being reported to the authorities and then dragged off to these "hospitals."

The people in Wuhan believed that they were being taken away to die and dumped into mass graves, in order that the government could more quickly kill the virus, rather than save the people! They did not believe or trust that these large buildings were really hospitals at all, at first, because they only saw people go in and not come out. They were scared.

Such an account is raw and as we move on, we'll discover both the rumours and the facts, in order to separate fact from fiction. And in an era of FAKE NEWS it turns out that there is no bigger FAKER than the CCP.

China's Fake Coronavirus Figures

According to Tucker Carlson, who calls out the world's media for being complicit in much of this, *(along with WHO's Director General Tedros Adhanom Ghebreyesus and many others);* **"When this pandemic finally recedes, the global order likely will be reset. Up for grabs will be control of the world - international financial systems, trade agreements, military alliances, shipping lanes. China would like to run all of it."**

He goes on to say, that at this point it's not a prize the Chinese can take by force. They've got to make the case to the rest of the world, and that's exactly what they're doing now. We are competent, they are saying. They are buffoons. The numbers prove it. Time to knock America from its perch. That's the message from the Chinese government. That's what they're saying.

What's striking is how many in the West are helping them say it. At 10:00 a.m., on January 23rd 2020, Chinese authorities locked down the city of Wuhan, site, of course, of the first coronavirus outbreak. But by then it was too late. And then an estimated five million residents of Wuhan had already fled the city and dispersed around the world. In many cases, they brought the disease with them.

Duplicity and Criminal Incompetence

Within days, it was clear to anyone who was paying attention that the duplicity and the criminal incompetence of the Chinese government was likely going to kill a lot of people.

Yet, the World Health Organization took the opposite view. On February 3rd, the Director General of WHO announced that China was doing the best imaginable job fighting coronavirus:

> *During my visit to Beijing last week, I was so impressed in my meeting with President Xi and his detailed knowledge of the outbreak and for his personal leadership. And if it weren't for China's efforts, the number of cases outside China would have been very much higher. There is no reason for measures that unnecessarily interfere with international travel and trade.*
> *-- Director General of WHO:*
> *Tedros Adhanom Ghebreyesus*

"China is doing a great job." The messaging continued like that for weeks.

As the pandemic was building and spreading across the world, the World Health Organization busied itself casting China as the hero of the story. If it weren't for the efforts of the Chinese government, many more would die.

A Battle for Control of the World

The Chinese government sees this moment as a battle in the struggle for control of the world. They're not distracted by impeachment or debates over pronouns. They think in sweeping terms. That's their advantage. It could be our undoing.

Just six weeks later, as if by magic, China declared victory over the epidemic. And not surprisingly, the director of the World Health Organization was there to celebrate and to amplify the message:

Of course, we have good, good news today. Yesterday, Wuhan reported no new cases for the first time since the outbreak started. Wuhan provides hope for the rest of the world that even the most severe situation can be turned around.

-- Director General of WHO:
Tedros Adhanom Ghebreyesus

"Wuhan is the hope of the world," he said. Lost in this very familiar cycle was any discussion of whether or not China's much-touted health numbers are real. And the short answer is no, they are not real. Like so much that comes out of China, from vinyl handbags to official Human Rights reports, they are fake.

The question is, how fake are they? And that's not clear. Since January, Chinese media have been under tighter than usual government controls, and that's saying something. Journalists have been arrested. Social media platforms have been scrubbed. We don't have a lot of reliable information about what is happening there.

> *We do know that totalitarian governments are far more efficient at controlling populations than unruly democracies like ours. Once quarantine began in Wuhan, for example, there were reports of police locking entire families in their apartments from the outside, only to be discovered dead - all of them - weeks later.*
>
> *-- Tucker Carlson*

Let's use Common Sense for a Moment

Tactics like that will definitely slow the spread of an epidemic but by how much? That's the question. So let's use common sense for a moment...

Overall, the report claimed only 416 people in Beijing had been infected domestically. Of those, 394 had already been released from medical care. In other words, in a city of 22 million people, there are only 22 hospital patients in Beijing who contracted the coronavirus in China, the country where it started. So literally one out of every million people. Is that believable? Western media outlets believed it. They repeated that claim as fact.

The Chinese government clearly knew better than that. The very next day, China closed every movie theater in the country. This Monday, two days ago, authorities in Shanghai shut down the city's two most popular tourist attractions, the Shanghai Tower and the Oriental Pearl Tower, for an indefinite period. That is not the behavior of a government that believes it has tamed the outbreak. No. It's an expression of fear.

China is the largest country in the world. When the Chinese distort critical datasets - like how many people are infected or how many are dying - that directly affects how every other country in the world responds to the disease.

We may have wasted months assuming things about the coronavirus that were not true. There's a big cost to that. But more broadly, we should be concerned about what comes after this.

The Chinese government sees this moment as a battle in the struggle for control of the world, and *"The World Health Organisation is a lapdog to the powerful and sucked up to China during the coronavirus crisis. WHO's leadership tells us that China 'set the standard' for the response to the outbreak. Apparently, that standard includes disappearing doctors who tell the truth about it." -- Tucker Carlson*[2]

Definition of The World Health Organisation

An official definition of The World Health Organization (WHO) is as follows: The WHO is a specialized agency of the United Nations responsible for international public health... its main objectives ensure *"the attainment by all peoples of the highest possible level of health."* It is headquartered in Geneva, Switzerland, with six semi-autonomous regional offices and 150 field offices worldwide.

The WHO was established on the 7th of April 1948, which is commemorated as World Health Day. The first meeting of the World Health Assembly (WHA), the agency's governing body, took place on the 24th of July 1948. The WHO incorporated the assets, personnel, and duties of the League of Nations' Health Organization and the Office International d'Hygiène Publique including the International Classification of Diseases. Its work began in earnest in 1951 following a significant infusion of financial and technical resources.

The WHO's broad mandate includes advocating for universal healthcare, monitoring public health risks, coordinating responses to health emergencies, and promoting human health and well being.

It provides technical assistance to countries, sets international health standards and guidelines, and collects data on global health issues through the World Health Survey.

Its flagship publication, the *World Health Report* provides expert assessments of global health topics and health statistics on all nations. The WHO also serves as a forum for summits and discussions on health issues.

The WHO has played a leading role in several public health achievements, most notably the eradication of smallpox, the near-eradication of polio, and the development of an Ebola vaccine. Its current priorities include communicable diseases, particularly HIV/AIDS, Ebola, malaria and tuberculosis; non-communicable diseases such as heart disease and cancer; healthy diet, nutrition, and food security; occupational health; and substance abuse.[3]

What a noble sounding organisation, however once subverted by the CCP it has become a different animal. Let's take a closer look at this particular organisation and its controversial Director General Dr Tedros Adhanom Ghebreyesus and his infamous role *(widely accused for his cosy relationship with the CCP resulting in calculated missteps and deliberate inaction)* during the early outbreak of the Covid-19 crisis.

❖

CHAPTER 2

The Silver Lining

A Growing Impetus for Reform

I f Covid-19 has had any silver lining thus far, it's been the growing impetus for reform. Much has been exposed by this pandemic not least The World Health Organization (WHO) which has come under growing scrutiny, concerning whether it has acted responsibly with transparency and whether it has remained independent of political corruption and influence.

> *The United Nations is an evil force, a stench to my nostrils... I will shake the United Nations, I will abolish it, for it has done nothing but steel and bring corruption... The United Nations has housed Judas and now I have taken Judas out, and I am revealing the lie...*
> *-- Prophetic Word by Kim Clement, April 16th 2005[1]*

The single largest funder of this organization is the United States, which has chosen to use its leverage to bring much needed reform. WHO's role in the Covid-19 pandemic has long been in question and has finally resulted in the suspension of contribution funds by the U.S., that amounted to approximately $400 million per annum.

WHO's Director General is seen as being primarily responsible for major missteps and crucial timewasting delays; not least of which was the initial miss-classification of the pandemic right at the very onset.

A Continued Exposé of WHO's Director General Tedros Adhanom Ghebreyesus

It has long been recognized and widely documented that Mr Tedros Adhanom Ghebreyesus has had a chequered political past, which is now being used to *hold-his-feet-to-the-fire* and help uncover corruption at the WHO.

The Facts: According Jianli Yang, *(founder and president of Citizen Power Initiatives for China)*, Mr Tedros is a trained microbiologist who earned his MSc in the immunology of infectious diseases at the University of London. Eventually becoming Ethiopia's Minister of Health, serving between 2005 and 2012; from this position he moved on to become Ethiopia's Minister of Foreign Affairs and served between 2012 and 2016.

Consistent with the National Review's account, Tedros served on the executive committee of the Tigray People's Liberation Front *(TPLF)*, which was one of four ethnically based political parties making up the Ethiopian People's Revolutionary Democratic Front *(EPRDF)*. It was a brutal authoritarian regime that ruled Ethiopia with an iron fist between 1991 and 2019.

Ultimately however, Tedros sought to take his place as Director General of the World Health Organization. This occurred back in 2017 when he was initially met with some fierce opposition, due to his service towards and in defence of his own country's abusive regime, *(as well as his less than stellar record as Minister of Health).*

> *Health ministers from Algeria and numerous other nondemocratic countries endorsed Tedros' candidacy for Director General of the WHO. The World Health Assembly approved him for the post with an overwhelming 133 votes out of 185, despite strong opposition from many Ethiopians who knew his derisory domestic record. **China was a major backer of Tedros's candidacy, as was his own TPLF party, which spent millions of dollars on his campaign.***
>
> *-- Jianli Yang*
> *National Review*

It's easy at this point to see - especially from events like this just how the various narratives get started – which suggest China was deliberately involved in the spreading of this global pandemic. Amongst other motives, to slow down the world's economy for its own aggrandizement and to set a new world order. Sacrificing its own people in the process, like those in the densely populated province of Wuhan.

Conspiracy or not, China looks culpable at this point and if nothing else China has certainly been caught with its pants down! Engineering events – many years in advance – in order to prop up bad actors like Tedros, to advance their world domination agenda and cover up any evidence of corruption along the way. China has a long history of questionable dealings, spanning many decades, which continue to be exposed and increase the global appetite for radical systemic change.

No One was Paying Enough Attention - to China

To continue our exposé, Tedros eventually secured the coveted spot at the WHO, but not without a cloud of controversy overshadowing him, as his candidacy was tarred with allegations that while acting as Ethiopia's Minister of Health, he covered-up three major cholera outbreaks *(fatal epidemics)*. Classifying them as nothing more than Acute Watery Diarrhea *(AWD)* to avoid any negative impact on Ethiopian's tourism or the image of his party.

All of which bears a striking resemblance to his treatment of the novel coronavirus – all in the pursuit of keeping up appearances for CHINA *(you guessed it!)*

All of a sudden the world has conceded that China, the shrewd powerbroker and smooth operator has been weaving its influence and aggressively networking, while everyone was seduced by all those "shiny-objects" in the opposite direction! Hypnotized by drumbeats such as: **"RUSSIA, RUSSIA, RUSSIA / COLLUSION COLLUSION COLLUSION!"**

Evidently it's been far less about Russia, impeachment, Kavanagh, Christopher Steel's bogus dossier, BREXIT, *(blah, blah, blah)* and much more about cunning CHINA. I predict, that many more politicians, government officials, big business and corporations, including vast institutions *(etc.,)* will be found to have "colluded" with China, than ever with Russia.

Tedros Flatters Xi Jinping while Beijing Aggressively Censors Information to Downplay the Viral Outbreak in Wuhan

However, during the early stages of the outbreak, Tedros was seen on TV and across the internet corroborating Beijing's clumsy efforts to minimize the outbreak in Wuhan. His lavish praise of Xi Jinping's was widely broadcast as "transparent" and "responsible." Elaborating his comments further by proclaiming how China had set a "new standard for the world." All while China was aggressively covering up the virus and censoring information.

Besides this blunder, his earliest and most fatal error was his delay in and deliberate refusal of correctly categorizing this viral outbreak as a **"Public Health Emergency of International Concern."** Regardless of mounting international pressure, Tedros continued to postpone its rightful classification, then when he did so finally on January 30, 2020 his behaviour was very ambassadorial in China's favour, assuring the world community that it wasn't, *"a vote of no confidence in China.*

On the contrary, WHO continues to have the confidence in China's capacity to control the outbreak." This served later only to feed the growing narrative that Tedros and WHO in general were China-centric and *"in the bag."*

Inaccurate Numbers

Numbers coming out of China early on were inaccurate, placing the number of deaths from the virus at just 361 *(which later was debunked and proven to be much higher)*. Tedros, however is on record at this point continuing to echo the chief sentiments and talking points coming out of China and remained resolutely opposed to putting any restrictions in place that would *"unnecessarily interfere with international trade and travel."* In retrospect, turns out this would have significantly slowed the outbreak's spread.

Late into February and just slightly prior to when the true extent of the pandemic's global impact was realized, WHO and its now infamous Director General were still in official opposition to any restrictive measures. The Chinese government *(Chinese Communist Party - CCP)* then proceeded in opportunely criticizing nations in particular *(who'd chosen to impose travel bans on China regardless)*, as being in violation of WHO's official advice.

Tedros' Cosy Relationship with China

As a result of Tedros' defiance of the facts and his cosy relationship with China *(the veritable lapdog)*, many in the global community are now calling for his ouster. *(Others say that ousting Tedros in the middle of a pandemic would not be sensible and that apportioning blame at this crucial juncture is not helpful)*.

To continue my point, there were many other countries who accepted the CCP's and WHO's line of enquiry and so did nothing to implement stricter border controls for themselves. Effortlessly infection rates soared between countries and death tolls rose as this pandemic became relentless. Even those nations who'd more wisely chosen to put travel restrictions in place were not immune.

Nothing could stop this runaway train with a cargo of death, despair and plague. It had zero regard for borders; social, political or otherwise. Random politicians, athletes, famous movie stars, social media influencers and celebrities, along with members of the royal family were all becoming infected. EVERYONE was impacted and NONE were immune.

However many silver linings emerge during wartime. When everyone is in the same boat, and no one enjoys immunity, a great sense of SOLIDARITY sets in. The best of humanity gets to rise and we all feel warmed by our renewed faith in humanity. Wartime heroes emerge and people bond forever.

Taiwan's Early Warnings

For now we continue talking about our current villain Dr Tedros, who it is believed was very well informed early on in the crisis but left life saving action untaken and truth unheeded. The key event to mention here is that by December 31, 2019, scientists in Taiwan *(which according to an article written in the National Review continues to be excluded from the WHO due to Chinese pressure)* notified WHO officials of evidence regarding "human-to-human" transmission, but the officials did not pass this information on to other countries.

So without any official acknowledgment or assistance from the WHO, Taiwan eventually managed better than most countries *(despite its relative proximity to Beijing compared to others)*. Likely because long-term distrust for the CCP was already well baked-in and so weren't duped by the propaganda coming out of Beijing to minimize the virus.

The International Community

No sooner had the world roused to the real threat of Covid-19, Tedros began openly accusing the international community, for his own earlier missteps and inaction! It was not until March 11, 2020, that Tedros finally classified the virus as a global pandemic so all the irony was not lost, when he finally pointed his finger reproachfully to say that, *"some countries were struggling with a lack of resolve."* That they were all, "deeply concerned" at the World Health Organization by the *"alarming levels of inaction."*

His duplicitous rants also claimed that "certain countries" were not "approaching the threat with the level of political commitment needed to control it," amounting to nothing more than disingenuous rhetoric.

So, as we take a glance at China's global ambitions, that include acts of subversion, espionage and much more, we find that unfolding before us, in the very throes of a pandemic, the real crisis going on behind the curtain. There is the toxic mixture of political theatre, corruption, racketeering, behaviours of dictators and despots and their authoritarian regimes. The likes of which Dr Tedros and others *(in various corridors of power)* are willing to do their bidding, coddling them and whitewashing their crimes.

Tedros' Coddling of Dictators

In October 18, 2017, only three months into his tenure as Director General, Tedros appointed Zimbabwe's Robert Mugabe, one of the longest-ruling and most brutal dictators on the planet, to serve as a WHO goodwill ambassador focused on tackling non-communicable diseases in Africa. "I am honored to be joined by President Mugabe of Zimbabwe, a country that places universal health coverage and health promotion at the center of its policies to provide healthcare to all," he said at a conference in Uruguay announcing the decision. But after the appointment was widely condemned by influential leaders in the health sector, politicians, and human-rights defenders, he eventually rescinded it.

-- Jianli Yang
National Review

Tedros's behaviour in the whole Covid-19 fiasco has been influenced by his penchant for dictators. His actions are self evident and well documented, *(thanks to investigative journalists who actually do their job, getting to the bottom of matters and holding truth to power)*. Reciprocal backscratching has been on display for all to see. It's been an open secret that the CCP and Tedros have shared common interests for decades.

The Facts: While still Ethiopia's Foreign Minister the CCP made extensive openhanded donations to the country, then equally supported Tedros' campaign for the top post at WHO. My question then has to be this: What exactly is Mr Tedros to the Chinese – simply a *"useful political idiot"* or one of many powerful international partners of the CCP?

It has been seen in Chinese state media how China has forcefully defended Tedros with claims that he's only being criticized by the West for helping China and not for his poor handling of the situation. Where China is chiefly responsible, Tedros is clearly not exempt. China's secrecy and censoring efforts for example stopped crucial information from spearing many lives; while Tedros has been proven complicit in assisting the cover up.

Subverting the World Health Organization, along with many other international institutions, has long been on China's radar. But Tedros' own inaction massively jeopardized an incalculable number of lives worldwide and the call for his ouster is undoubtedly legitimate.[2]

When & Why Trump Stopped WHO's Funding

Timeline: The following is a brief timeline that concerns escalating tensions between U.S. President Donald Trump and Director General Tedros Adhanom Ghebreyesus of the World Health Organisation [WHO]. With emphasis on the word "WORLD." This is a UN organisation but is not meant to be selective about which countries it deems to be included in the "WORLD" *(Taiwan for example)*.

You've probably discovered by now, that the WHO are typically a propaganda machine *(particularly during Tedros' tenure)*, which essentially provides the "party-line" *(for the*

CCP). AND it is well established that the world's media and other interested parties simply check-in with the WHO's official "talking points" but clearly not for the "facts," *(too many blunders caused WHO to haemorrhage too much of its credibility).*

April 7, 2020
Trump criticized the WHO for mishandling the pandemic. ***"The WHO really blew it. For some reason, funded largely by the United States, yet very China-centric. We will be giving that a good look. Fortunately, I rejected their advice on keeping our borders open to China early on. Why did they give us such a faulty recommendation?"***

April 8
"Please don't politicize this virus," Tedros said in a briefing in Geneva after he was asked about Trump's remarks the day before. He later urged political leaders to *"please quarantine politicizing COVID."*

April 14
"Today I am instructing my administration to halt funding of the World Health Organization while a review is conducted to assess the World Health Organization's role in severely mismanaging and covering up the spread of the coronavirus," Trump said in a briefing at the White House.

April 15
"We regret the decision of the president of the United States to order a halt in funding to the World Health

Organization," said Tedros at a news conference. Responding to the U.S. accusations, Ryan of the WHO said, *"In the first weeks of January, the WHO was very, very clear."*

"We alerted the world on January the 5th," Ryan said. *"Systems around the world, including the U.S., began to activate their incident management systems on January the 6th. And through the next number of weeks, we've produced multiple updates to countries, including briefing multiple governments, multiple scientists around the world, on the developing situation — and that is what it was, a developing situation."*

In an interview with NPR on April 16, the U.S. ambassador to the United Nations, Kelly Craft, stated: **"[The World Health Organization] was not accurate. Had it been accurate, it would have slowed the virus and saved thousands of lives."**[3]

Will the U.S. Finally & Completely Terminate It's Membership with the UN?

Not much love has been lost between the States and the UN in recent times, yet this is not likely to change any time soon. Although it's been a long time coming and within this new era of "impetus for reform," anything's possible. We must not forget however that the U.S. *(and Israel)* already withdrew from the United Nations Educational, Scientific and Cultural Organization *(UNESCO)* back in 2017 and the United Nations Human Rights Council *(UNHRC)* in 2018.

Though one of its founding members, there are still calls for the U.S. to leave the United Nations Security Council as well. Proposals for which have long come from typical quarters that view the UN as a threat to America's sovereignty or who go with the theory that the U.N. is a potential world government.

Either way, change is in the air and if prophecy is correct, the UN will be abolished at some point anyway *(see various prophecies by Kim Clement within this book series, who repeatedly spoke of the UN's demise).*[4]

❖

CHAPTER 3

A New Autocratic Culture

Ushering in the Socialist Agenda

I will start this particular chapter telling you about my own family's battle with this novel coronavirus. You might already be wondering what that might have to do with China? Well, nothing and yet everything. Because our beloved Italy is fast becoming just another surveillance state.

As Britons, we just came through a monumental period called Brexit (by no small measure). And what an epic battle that was! Involving many more countries than just Britain. However, like much else, it was put on hold during the pandemic, yet still, history was made. There was no going back. The British public had had enough.

Our vote, like so many, was cast during the referendum and therefore, we have a voice. We did not remain silent. We engaged in the debate and we voted. Too many want an opinion, without voting. But if you don't vote, then quite honestly, your opinion doesn't count.

There's No Voting Going On!

However, much of what is going on is **ushering in the socialist agenda,** let there be no bones about that. And there is no due process going on - zero voting. It is all being decided autocratically. Much is being decided without the public have any say whatsoever. This is, chilling. Governments have more autocratic power now, after this pandemic than they ever had before and don't think they will relinquish it. They won't.

We are all steadily becoming more and more like China. The drones fly over our homes daily and much more. But perhaps most shocking, is the fact that here in Italy *(a veritable mecca for Catholicism)* it is banned to go to church. This year we have head to postpone our graduation ceremony, until some time in the unforeseeable future, because everything is up in the air and gatherings, especially church centric ones are BANNED. And there's nothing polite about it.

It's irreligious. It's all about the science and yet much of the science has been confused or debunked. This is eerily reminiscent of every other totalitarian regime and its small beginnings. Yet there's nothing small about this.

All roads lead to China and I will explain to you the *Belt and Road Initiative* that China has poured money into for decades and for why.

My Family's Personal Battle with Covid-19

For now, let's get personal and draw you in to my family's experience with this disease. Something I wish China had kept to itself. I am not being pedantic or facetious. But no synthetic virus is welcome in my home again. No thank you China. No thank you CCP. But let us *all* receive fair warning; this is not over with Covid-19, its only just beginning. If this is what China can do, then the CCP is just flexing its muscles, and regardless of mounting international pressures, China is out to exert its strength on the world and make its long awaited power grab for world domination. BUT let's read on:

Not even Beautiful Tuscany was Immune

Here I live in the very heart of Europe with my lovely English family, in Tuscany Italy, where now they are rolling out a new tracking app of all things. At first it was just a rumour, now it is a reality, with emphasis on stopping a second wave infection. Fear motivates. Ask me how I know. Our little girl and my youngest child, had the virus and couldn't breathe properly for an entire month. She got better and then relapsed. At night she could have died in her sleep because she was unable to breath without help.

So I am not aloof by far, to the realities of these symptoms. They are real and we got up close and personal with them. It was not good at all. Her persistent fevers, her lungs full, her heart beating so fast it would not calm down, her eye balls were hurting, notwithstanding her whole body was in pain, all her joints and so forth. She would not eat and was deathly pale. Symptoms we had not witnessed before. But we had some heavy duty prayer support from friends all around the world and for that my wife and I will forever be grateful. It was a battle. Not one I want to fight again.

We had no official test done, because they weren't available and not offered but we were in constant communication with our paediatric who was very serious. We were ordered to stay at home and without any official help our daughter was healed. All the credit for our daughter's healing belongs only to the Lord.

When Medicines don't Work

The doctor tried antibiotics but that did not seem to help for obvious reasons. So our hands were not tied, they were in the Lord's and He came through as He always has. *(To Jesus be the glory forever and ever, amen).*

Staying at home meant we did not have to take her into the hospitals that were already filled to capacity and overflowing *(not safe places to be).* So let it be understood, loud and clear, that this battle with the novel coronavirus Covid-19 has been a real one for my family and I. AND I am not writing about something I have been untouched by. It is not all rhetoric and conjecture. And naturally on a purely human level I can sympathise with any who have suffered and lost loved ones. Absolutely!

However, our faith is in Jesus Christ and we know that our house is built on Solid Rock. When the shaking comes (and it will), we shall be found standing! There is going to be more of this unrest and recalibration of the world order. I truly believe that we've seen nothing yet *(mark my words).*

BUT should we lay down in defeat and just take whatever comes? NO. Of course not! We fight on a different battlefield. Therefore we must know how to pray (2 Corinthians 10:4).

Justifiable Surveillance?

The tracking app that Italy has now adopted is called "Immuni" *(its moniker has obvious connotations),* and it should send chills down anyone's spine. I will keep this brief but China's fingerprints are all over this, yet again. The whole idea has emerged from China and has been reengineered by other countries to fit their own purposes.

There are few surprises left. We all know that the drones, which police are using around the world, are called **"UAVs - Unmanned Aerial Vehicles"** they are not new. Such devices are also made in and supplied by China of course, *(but we will get to that!)* YET, the whole world has witnessed the behaviour of some southern Italian Mayors, who have arbitrarily chased down random walkers, *(screaming expletives and obscenities at them),* scaring them half to death.

I perceive by this, that too many people in positions of power have now been triggered. It's in their fallen nature to want to control others. Power happy Mayors *(triggered by this whole Covid-19 dilemma),* will not quietly yield back to inertia. They have been exercised and will find no occasion to revert back to what was.

Heavy Surveillance - there's always a Trade Off

I've covered City Brain, for example, in some of my other materials, concerning the heavy surveillance practices of entire cities within China, but for now Immuni is our target issue. Why chills? Because our civil liberties are about to disappear for good! It's hard to imagine, especially as protests begin to build across the globe, *(clearly not everyone is ready to comply)*. But after a battery round of pandemic-like attacks, relentless germ warfare or bioterrorism, then we'll see just how quickly people consent or relinquish for a price *(because there's always a trade off)*.

When people are punch-drunk by the circumstances and battle-fatigued, it's innate and coded within our DNA to rely on the basic instinct that overrides all others, *"self-preservation."* It's ugly in the best of us, and yet we are hardwired it would seem, even retrofitted, with this instinct. *(It takes something greater than us - living within - to overcome these baser instincts, 1 John 4:4).*

Helicopters and Drones

Democracy is in decline and socialism is on the rise – that is clear. BUT I still don't think we should overestimate socialism or underestimate democracy quite so quickly, just yet.

I can tell you that we already have drones and helicopters flying over our home, quite regularly, especially during the shutdown. April is the month of Easter celebrations and helicopters were taking footage of us and not being too discrete about it either. *(Our hometown is so benign and tranquil with little crime, so who would consider such draconian measures necessary?)*

When it comes to infringements on our civil liberties, just consider that during lock down, people in various cities around the world, were permitted to hold protests, buy weed and even have an abortion, but they were strictly forbidden to attend their local churches! Shock and awe *should* be our reaction. BUT we are becoming anesthetised. So, what will it be like in two years from now?

Coercion & Fear

An epic pandemic of this magnitude has the power to coerce millions of people to give up their last vestiges of privacy in the name of fear and protection. We have mocked China's authoritarianism and draconian ways for many decades but now those "ways" are slowly becoming ours too.

I have long believed in China's take over bid for the rest of the world and that it was just a matter of time. A *"time"* none more evident than right *"now"* and many other discerning voices are joining the same chorus. BUT is it already too late?

Watch as Propaganda Employs Both Anger and Fear To Drive Home an Effective Narrative

I don't believe anything has to be too late, in this context. Yet I am convinced that nothing will ever be "normal" again, once this event subsides. It was designed to usher in a whole new way of thinking and there is no going back.

The governments of this world have powerful leverages at their disposal. How else can they successfully control people in democratic societies, without causing uprisings?

(Unless that's the plan!) Fear or anger are the two biggest motivators. For example, its usually fear for our own safety and anger against the machine *(perceived injustice)*.

❖

CHAPTER 4

It's all about the "Science"

Making a Mockery of the Stay at Home Order

Many times conservatives and Christians *(evangelicals in particular)* are labelled as *"science deniers,"* which is not a moniker we all deserve. Yet, it's mud that tends to stick, simply due to the fact that we *(generally speaking)* aren't always so skilful in the art of apologetics, so that we may defend our faith or worldview. BUT we are getting better at it. Much better. And the more informed we become, the better we will be.

Weaponizing the Science or Making it a Religion

"Science-denier" is a derogatory term that suggests Christians are troglodytes *(knuckle dragging cave men and women, of the stone age)* who are still primitive *(uneducated)* and therefore superstitious and ignorant. So, while a "paleo" diet is vastly popular these days, a Palaeolithic attitude is not. We are far too sophisticated. However, the worship of science is the other extreme, yet science has indeed become its own religion.

Controlling the flow of information is vital to those looking to achieve ultimate population control. Weaponizing the "science" is another way to control our thinking. Here's a short list of contradictory misinformation we received from the beginning:

- *Travel / don't travel*
- *Take cruises / don't take cruises - (famous early missteps)*
- *Yes masks / no masks*
- *Yes gloves / no gloves*
- *Stay indoors / stay outdoors (sunlight kills the virus etc.)*
- *Cluster / don't cluster*
- *Gather / don't gather*
- *Go to the supermarket / don't go to church*
- *Go to an Abortion Clinic / Still don't go to church*
- *Buy weed & alcohol – they're "essential"*
- *Sweden's got it right / Sweden's reckless*

  (The WHO couldn't make up their mind about Sweden and suffered self-contradiction in the process).
- *Much more could be added to this list and discussed... my point is where's the science in this list!*

Was the Stay at Home Lockdown a Mockery?

Quarantine is when you restrict movement of sick people. Tyranny is when you restrict the movement of healthy people… Every person has learned a harsh lesson about social distancing. We don't need a nanny state to tell people how to be careful.

-- Meshawn Maddock[1]

The CCP virus appears to weaken or die more readily when exposed to increasing amounts of sunlight, heat, or humidity.

-- William Bryan

If it's true that Covid-19 *"survives best in indoor and dry conditions, and is less able to survive in hotter, more humid conditions"* why then was the shutdown necessary, when we needed to be in the sunshine all along? Did the scientists get it wrong; was the stay at home order a scientific misstep? We are always led to believe that science is *"exact"* and doesn't make mistakes. The contradicting misinformation was deliberate then?

Our most striking observation today is the powerful effect that solar light appears to have on killing the virus — both on surfaces and in the air… We've seen a similar effect with both temperature and humidity as well, where increasing the temperature or the humidity or both is generally less favourable to the virus… The virus dies quickest in the presence of direct sunlight.

-- William Bryan

Applied Science & Practical Application

"Increased temperature, humidity, and sunlight are detrimental to SARS-CoV-2 in saliva droplets on surfaces and in the air... For nonporous surfaces such as steel, in a dark and low-humidity environment, the CCP virus has an 18-hour half-life — the time required for it to decrease by half, according to the researchers' findings.

*The half-life drops to six hours if the humidity is increased, with all other factors controlled. And when sunlight is further added to the equation, **the half-life drops to about two minutes.***

*For aerosol-type conditions, such as when people cough or sneeze, the virus has a half-life of about an hour in dark, low-humidity conditions. Adding direct sunlight, however, decreases the virus's half-life to **one and a half minutes...**" He went on to say that there are "many unknown links in the COVID-19 transmission chain, the trends observed so far can support practical decision-making to curb the spread of the CCP virus."[2]*
-- Mimi Nguyen Ly, April 24th 2020

This is exactly my point, if we are given the correct information and the correct science, at the correct time, then we can self regulate. We can use common sense that has been correctly informed. But governmental "over reach" that descends into the *"nanny state"* – assumes that we are all stupid and reckless and can't be trusted. Decision-making is taken out of our hands and autonomy dies. This would be the beginning of tyranny and people are right to be concerned about that.

The definition of a nanny state is when governments are authoritarian, overprotective and excessively handholding. Especially when they interfere, improperly, with personal choice.

There is no such thing as *"personal"* or *"private"* in communism, which we discuss at length, later on. BUT concepts like these are what China and other countries are built on:

Abolish all private property.

– Karl Marx

Actually China's aspirations exceed communism, more recently it has exposed itself as a fascist state *(I qualify this statement later on),* a state that doesn't want to abolish *"some"* private property but *"all"* private property.

This includes intellectual property, thoughts, beliefs and ideas. AND all things promoting *"individualism"* are seen as selfish and abolished. The *"individual"* literally becomes *"property"* of the state. This is the ultimate direction that certain world governments are going in right now and China is not alone, *(history proves otherwise).*

❖

CHAPTER 5

A Different Battle Field

New War Games

People in the West don't have the stomach for war and China knows that, so it adapts to a different battlefield. There's no need for atom bombs anymore. Sure we will always stockpile them. The Cold War took care of that. In fact, what it relied on then it still relies on now - the official term "M.A.D" (*"Mutually Assured Destruction"*).

My point? Everyone loses in warfare like that. World governments (*and organised crime syndicates like the Mafia*), say to themselves, "Why use such destructive force when you can be more sophisticated and more effective using cyber warfare, germ warfare, bioterrorism, and so on." You can literally wipe out entire enemy armies using infectious diseases. Silent killers are more cost effective because they don't use bullets!

China assumes that it is always much smarter than everyone else (the adult in the room), especially when it comes to politics, and its goal of removing the competition, is a ruthless one. For example by flooding the markets of its competitors with cheap, accessible and highly addictive drugs. Not to the underbelly of society but to the middle class! Painkillers like fentanyl and others, which have had a devastating impact on regular society.

The Enemy Within – The Trojan Manipulator

China is the enemy within. The Trojan horse if you like. It seeks to destroy its enemy from within. And what better way, than to get your enemy to destroy himself? What better strategy! Plus, by using subversion of long-standing institutions like Church organisations, and Universities *(the entire education system)*, then China can alter the fabric of our very culture.

Whether it's industry, technology, engineering, medical, the military, the police, the arts, education, religion, the sports, China has infiltrated it ALL, but in stealth you ask? No! In broad daylight because we weren't paying enough attention.

Most of this is self-inflicted, I wager, because companies have out-sourced their products to China too much. Take Apple for instance; my own MacBook Pro was designed by Apple in the United States, but made in China. Actually most products are *"made in China."* And over the years we've just assumed this as insignificant; just a matter of cheap labour perhaps and not given it any more thought. BUT if China makes EVERYTHING, doesn't that put us in a bad spot? And isn't it likely that they would copy, adapt and help-themselves to vast amounts of intellectual property *(designs etc.)*, especially when they've already gotten their hands on it? *(it's counterintuitive)*.

Why have countries been so trusting towards this totalitarian government? How have we been so seduced by what we say we oppose? We are a contradiction to ourselves, are we not?

In addition we hear proven reports and warnings that police drones, which have been used in the West for years *(but made in China)*, have been sending important data back to China. Of course! *(This stuff reads like a poor political novel. It's all so predictable – it's painful!)*

Democracy "Procrastinates" while China "Dominates"

While China sets its long-term goals, as an autocratic government, our more democratic countries in the West just keep kicking the can down the street, hoping for the *"next"* government in line to come and "fix" what we didn't. In this system little gets "fixed" and there are few long-term benefits gained. China on the other hand, wheels and deals and is relentlessly "fixing," *(quietly in the background)*.

While democracy chases its own tail, makes a lot of noise and is unbearably unpredictable, totalitarianism *(a system of one-party-rule that tolerates no rebellion),* zero confusion reigns. Everyone toes the line *(and everyone feels the OPPRESSION!)* But when it comes to getting things done, China gets things done.

Italy's Government is a "Fragile" Hot Mess

China exploits the mess of others. Take Italy for example, why is this government so fragile? Why the constant collapse and turnover, why the political revolving door? What LONG TERM benefits could possibly come from such instability? *(What fruit can be born from a tree that keeps uprooting itself every 15 months or so?)* What can grow or last in this environment?

Part of the problem is Italy's lack of faith in government, contributing to rebellion and high levels of tax evasion *(a massive black market economy).* However the authors of Italy's 1946 constitution were wary of a system that could put too much power into the hands of a single figure, like **Benito Mussolini,** who ruled Italy from 1922 to 1943, and who led Italy into World War II.

Yet this resulted in a weak parliamentary system, forcing heads of governments to use risky confidence votes to pass reforms. If a leader loses a confidence vote, he and his entire government are required to step down.

In addition, this constant state of flux is not helped by its fractured nature, *"Italy has too many political parties, too many conflicting interests,"* Arianna Montanari, a sociologist and political scientist at Rome's La Sapienza University. *"The more interests there are the more difficult it is for them to work together."*[1]

Do I advocate for and am I in favour of socialism or communism? No, by no means. I don't favour espionage, super surveillance, tracking, spying, cyber terrorism, identity theft, steeling of intellectual property, bioterrorism, and long-term mining of data both personal and corporate and on and on. China had divulged itself into it all to coerce, seduce even blackmail, not just high-ranking officials but entire governments and countries.

China doesn't intend to Play Fair nor does the Devil

When we are duped into voluntarily surrendering our own freedoms to save ourselves from any discomfort or embarrassment, then we are easily controlled and no war is ever necessary. It's a genius move. *(Lull us into a state of fixed and false security - a stupor so close to a state of sleep - then steel the baby from our arms. It's diabolical).*

The Tracking APP called Immuni

The Facts: From a European viewpoint, tracking is not unique to us. But on April 17th The Local news outlet and other sources confirmed that Italy has announced the first details of its plan to use an app to trace coronavirus infections, as it looks at easing its two-month lockdown in early May.

Coronavirus commissioner Domenico Arcuri signed a decree late on Thursday (April 16, 2020) awarding the Mediterranean country's contract to a Milan-based startup called Bending Spoons. The app, named Immuni, was chosen from over 300 proposals sent to the Ministry of Innovation... The European Union recommended smartphone tracking apps as part of a roadmap unveiled on Wednesday to help countries ease restrictions that have prompted steep economic downturns across the bloc.

*The Italian app is based on Bluetooth, in accordance with the EU's recommendations against using geo-location. It stated that all apps used for this purpose should be used **anonymously and voluntarily.** Arcuri's decree in turn states that the free app must preserve users' anonymity and not track location. Instead, it will use Bluetooth to log the phone's movements. The plan is to test the app in pilot regions and then expand it nationally. No timeframes were disclosed.*

Italy's announcement came a week after Apple and Google revealed plans to develop a contact-tracing app. Their initiative would allow apps on phones using rival Apple and Google-backed Android software to exchange information.

*Countries such as South Korea and Israel have used apps to help people determine whether they came close to someone infected with the virus. Technology experts warn that such apps are not fool proof since Bluetooth signals work best in open spaces and can be dropped in walled-off offices and restaurants. Italy has officially recorded 22,170 deaths from the virus, and is now looking to **gradually lift its restrictions from May 4.**[2]*

This was confirmed by Alessio Iannicelli from The Patent who said, "Italy is preparing for Phase 2. For several days now, the Italian government has been working to organize, define and optimize the reopening of production activities and the return (hopefully) to normal after the lockdown imposed by the Coronavirus emergency…" And of the tracking app he said, "The Immuni app will not be mandatory: only those who want to use it can download it for free from Android or IOS stores."

Contact Tracking & Immuni
Have we been Immunized to all the Risks?

The chills I spoke of a while ago, should be increasing down your spine right about now. Why? Because in the name of science, we are being asked to give up ALL of our rights, and those of our children! This is beyond dangerous. Technology that knows EVERYTHING about us, that can get into the wrong hands, has the potential to be very dangerous indeed.

It's a political hot potato! Hackers and bad actors with that kind of information in their hands are capable of doing anything and organized crime is becoming more "organized"!

People aren't mining for gold any more, but for information. Let me be abundantly clear: **INFORMATION IS THE NEW GOLD.** And regardless of the risks, we are expected to comply and *"support"* these governmental regulations and measures willingly. After all, you have nothing to hide, right? *(That's what they would say in Nazi Germany. Now does it bother you?)*

How Immuni Works

The Facts: Apparently the app will perform two major functions.

1. First, *Immuni will provide extensive contact tracking using Bluetooth technology. The system detects when two smartphones approach each other less than 1 meter away and keeps track of all contacts. In this way, if a person tests positive for the Coronavirus, it is possible to reconstruct all his or her contacts and track potential infected persons. All this in total anonymity: once downloaded, in fact, the Immuni app records contacts in the form of encrypted identification codes.*

2. The second function of Immuni *is a sort of "clinical diary" where each citizen can enter a series of relevant information (sex, age, previous illnesses, medication intake) and note any symptoms or changes in health status. The app will be "an important pillar in the management of the next phase of the emergency", explained Commissioner Arcuri.*

The Commissioner went on to make it clear that, before the app is made available, a trial will be launched in a number of pilot regions "to progressively extend the voluntary option, but we hope massive numbers of our citizens will be able to endure and support this system, which we need to avoid a repeat of the previous dramatic phase".[3]

The Internet isn't in the Cloud but Under the Oceans

Now, I know that much more could be said about this particular subject, but I just want to bring it in here. Because while we talk about safety online, who truly realizes that our data is actually under the sea!

With this in mind, it's not hard to see how hackers are actually under the oceans and not in the cloud, as many suppose. Mining sensitive information from submarines and seabed cables! Super information highways. Obviously such information is increasingly vulnerable, as hackers become more and more ingenious:

> *People think that data is in the cloud, but it's not... it's in the ocean.*
>
> *-- Jayne Stowell*

What a consideration! As Adam Satariano of the New York Times says, the Internet consists of tiny bits of code that move around the world, traveling along wires as thin as a strand of hair strung across the ocean floor. The data zips from New York to Sydney, from Hong Kong to London, in the time it takes you to read this word.

Nearly 750,000 miles of cable already connect the continents to support our insatiable demand for communication and entertainment. Companies have typically pooled their resources to collaborate on undersea cable projects, like a freeway for them all to share.[4]

❖

CHAPTER 6

Britain's China Policy

Huawei & The 5G Networks

By March 27th 2020, Britain's PM Boris Johnson had announced that he had tested positive for the CCP virus. Since taking office, he had been surrounded by fierce opposition on issues like Brexit, Britain's China policy, Huawei and its 5G networks – and not least - its *special* relations with the U.S.

Since first starting to write this book much has changed, yet even at the time of publishing events will still be unfolding. For example, I started writing in March 2020 and by April sentiments had altered. Was Boris flip-flopping over his original concrete decision concerning Huawei?

Was this due to mounting pressure or was Boris being threatened by China? *(Remember with multiple propaganda machines, pumping away, not everything we're being told is going to add up, perhaps you've noticed that already!)*

Speculation at the beginning of April had some headlines reading like this, *"Britain pulls out of 5G contract with Chinese firm Huawei after test kits were found contaminated with Corona virus."*

Yet exactly one month on, the speculation of major headlines had changed to read something like this one found in the Telegraph on May 4th which stated, *"U.S. spy planes could be pulled from Britain while the White House conducts major Huawei review… RC-135s could be at risk, after Britain lets Chinese telecom giant build its 5G network."*

Apparently, with a hint of betrayal in the air, the White House had already launched a major review at this point, to assess whether their spy planes *(the highly sophisticated reconnaissance aircrafts called RC-135s, yet considered most vulnerable)*, intelligence officials and other U.S. assets, needed to be pulled out of Britain after Downing Street agreed that Huawei can help build its 5G network.

The said *"review"* is predicted to have negative *"ramifications"* on the *"special relationship"* that's long existed between the U.S. and the UK, *(first coined by Winston Churchill back in 1946).*[1]

So Where does Boris Stand with the CCP & What are His Family's Ties with the Regime?

On January 28th, 2020 Boris Johnson essentially gave the green light to the CCP by announcing that Britain would permit *"high-risk suppliers"* to participate in the construction of the *"non-sensitive part"* of Britain's 5G network. While Huawei and Beijing would unquestionably have welcomed this move, it has received mounting opposition ever since, especially from existing allies who feel the bitter sting of betrayal:

> *Huawei insiders reveal that the company has close ties with the CCP, and has been accused of stealing from others to develop its own technology. The Trump administration has sought to convince allies to ban Huawei from 5G networks over security concerns. However, Johnson ignored the U.S. warning and concerns voiced by British lawmakers.*
>
> *-- The Epoch Times Editorial*

> *It's allowing the fox into the hen house when really we should be guarding the wire… This leaves many concerns and does not close the UK's networks to a frequently malign international actor.*
>
> *-- Tom Tugendhat, Conservative MP*

> *"I think the time has come for people to pick sides. The question is: are we to remain with the Western democracies that have always been our allies, or are we to throw our lot in with the Chinese Communist Party?" He added, "It's the worst decision any British government has made in years… It threatens the Five Eyes partnership, our prospects of a new trade agreement with the U.S. and Australia and perhaps even the future of NATO."*
>
> *-- Nigel Farage, Brexit Party Leader*

I'm calling for a thorough review of U.S.-U.K. intelligence-sharing... I fear London has freed itself from Brussels only to cede sovereignty to Beijing... it's like allowing the KGB to build its telephone network during the Cold War.

-- Tom Cotton (R-Ark.),
Member of the U.S. Senate Intelligence Committee

Nigel Farage - The Enlightened One!

Nigel Farage is an interesting fellow who's spent decades, battling away in Brussels, that it's made him a bit of a seer. He's seen too much and knows too much, to just go politely away and shut up! AND he's one of those people you can't help but listen to. He doesn't vomit empty rhetoric like so many others. When he speaks, he actually says something. However, for some he's easy to underestimate. BUT I would advice; don't write him off so quickly.

"We didn't free Britain from Brussels only to bow before Beijing. Conservatives must rebel over Huawei."
*Elsewhere he added, "Sadly, under Boris Johnson's regime, not much appears to have changed. Just look at one of our key strategic industries, British Steel. It appears to have been sold to another Chinese firm, Jingye, despite competitive bids from other parts of the world. **I believe that the same establishment that sold out our nation to the European Union is now selling us out to China.**"*

-- Nigel Farage

A Family Affair

Farage wrote an article in Newsweek back in February 2020 criticising Boris and his family, opposing his proposal to allow Huawei to help build Britain's 5G network and for getting too cosy with the CCP. Pointing out that Boris had been too influenced by too many *"pro-China"* figures including members of his own family!

Only a couple of weeks ago his father, Stanley, had a 90-minute meeting with the Chinese ambassador to London, Liu Xiaoming. Afterwards, Johnson Snr emailed UK officials outlining Xiaoming's worries that his son Boris had failed to send a personal message of support after the coronavirus outbreak. This fascinating insight only became public because Johnson Snr accidentally copied the BBC into his message...

*Then there is Boris's younger brother, Jo, who was Britain's Universities Minister until 2019. During his time in post, he endorsed the University of Reading's partnership **with China's Nanjing University, which specialises in — you guessed it — information, science and technology.***

-- Farage's Newsweek article
February 2020

Not only that, but Farage also revealed that the PM's step-brother Max also has close ties with the Chinese regime. According to public information, Max Johnson got his MBA from Beijing University before working for Goldman Sachs in Hong Kong. He is now running his own investment company, which caters to firms that sell products to China.[2]

Huawei – One of Beijing's Chief Tools in its Efforts For World Domination

I've seen the best and worst of China… if a company like Huawei is asked to cooperate with Chinese State Security spies, its executives simply can't say no.

-- Nick Kristof

Huawei is one of the most strategic tools China has to help in its efforts to master the universe! AND Britain, aware of the security risks with Huawei said that they saw such risks as *"manageable."* Is this folly, naivety or just a, *"better the devil you know,"* kind of policy?

Either way, such endorsement of the firm has ensured that its decade long expansion went unhindered, that by September 2019 already, it was revealed that Huawei had set up its new artificial intelligence (AI) research laboratory in London, with an estimated 200 AI research engineers. As part of the firms *"OpenLab"* network and by December of the same year *Huawei's 5G Innovation and Experience Centre* was officially *"unveiled."*

Johnson's Very Pro-China Posturing

We are very enthusiastic about the Belt and Road Initiative. We are very interested in what President Xi is doing…

-- Boris Johnson 2019

Eager to advertise Britain as an *"open economy,"* Boris said: *"Don't forget [we are] the most open international investment [destination], **particularly [for] Chinese investment**. We have Chinese companies coming in to Hinkley, for instance, the big nuclear power plant."*

Cosy Relations with the CCP

According to Tian Yun of The Epoch Times, "In October 2013 Johnson led a trade delegation as the, then Mayor of London, to go to China for a six-day visit. They met with China's top entrepreneurs, major investors, and high-ranking officials, hoping to establish a closer cooperative relationship with China.

During his term as mayor, he promoted a partnership between London and Shanghai, two financial hubs. On June 17, 2019, the China Securities Regulatory Commission and Financial Conduct Authority of the United Kingdom made a joint announcement of their approval of the new Shanghai-London Stock Connect. On the same day, the inauguration ceremony was held in London.

The Shanghai-London Stock Connect

According to the rules, eligible companies listed on the Shanghai Stock Exchange would be able to issue Global Depository Receipts (GDRs) to the UK and global investors and apply for them to be listed on the London Stock Exchange's Main Market. Eligible companies listed on the London Stock Exchange would be able to issue Chinese Depository Receipts (CDRs) to Chinese investors and apply for them to be listed on the Main Board of the Shanghai Stock Exchange.

Some commentators pointed out that the establishment of the Shanghai-London Stock Connect is tantamount to a *'blood transfusion'* to support the CCP.

Post Brexit UK-China Relations

After the Johnson administration left the European Union, it naturally needed to find new trade partners. On the one hand, the UK maintains its friendship with the United States, but it is also eager to strengthen economic and trade ties with China. China has become its second largest trading partner outside the EU. From January to August 2018, the bilateral trade volume between China and Britain was as high as $51.05 billion.

From January to August 23, 2019, Chinese companies completed 15 major acquisitions in the UK, worth approximately $8.3 billion. For example, Alibaba's Ant Financial acquired London-headquartered payments company World First in February. Hillhouse Capital acquired the shares of the Scotch whisky brand Loch Lomond Group for 400 million pounds in June and became its largest shareholder.

*In September last year, the Hong Kong Stock Exchange attempted to acquire the London Stock Exchange for $36.6 billion, but was rejected. The Chinese government is the largest shareholder of the Hong Kong Stock Exchange and holds 6 seats among its 13 board members. **It is*** *foreseeable that if the acquisition was successful, the CCP would have control of the entire European financial market.*

Human Rights Record

On January 2, 2020, five sources told Reuters that the Chinese regime temporarily suspended the Shanghai-London Connect plan because of the British stance on Hong Kong's pro-democracy protests and the UK's response to the detention of a former employee of the British Consulate in Hong Kong. The next day, the China Securities Regulatory Commission nonetheless claimed that Shanghai-London Connect was not affected.

In fact, the CCP is accustomed to using economic interests as a bargaining chip—to coerce Western governments and commercial enterprises to remain silent about the CCP's violation of human rights.

Perhaps Johnson has not yet realized that the path of economic and trade cooperation with the CCP is extremely unstable. Any nation that partners with the CCP may be forced to give up its conscience at a certain point."

The Epoch Times editorial article, "Where Ties With Communist China Are Close, the Coronavirus Follows," points out that the CCP virus specifically targets the Chinese regime and those who support it. The spread of the virus around the world shows that countries and regions with close ties to the CCP have been seriously affected. The CCP is evil in nature. I hope Boris Johnson will learn a lesson from his illness and reflect on his policies.[3]

❖

CHAPTER 7

Chinese Communist Ties Suffer Most from Covid-19

China's Lured Foreign Investment

It has to be said that the heaviest-hit places outside China all share one common thread - their close and lucrative ties to the communist rule in Beijing.

Many foreign entities, politicians, and organizations have come under enough pressure from the CCP that they have been persuaded to look the other way or comply with pernicious behaviour and unspeakable crimes committed by the ruling party.

*Recent decades have seen the PRC greatly expand its power in economic and geopolitical affairs. Deceiving the world with a narrative of **"China's peaceful rise,"** the* *communist regime has lured foreign governments and international firms to invest in China's rapidly developing markets.*

But the CCP has never abandoned its ideological tenets of class struggle and totalitarian control. In the 30 years since the Tiananmen Square massacre, and from the start in 1999 of the persecution of the spiritual practice Falun Gong to today's **systematic persecution of all faiths and independent thought,** *the state of human rights in the PRC has only worsened.*

Italy Suffered for her Close Ties to China

Apparently since 2004, *"more than 350 million people have renounced their ties to the Party and its affiliated youth organizations."* On the contrary, those who have aligned themselves with the CCP and its communism have reaped the consequences. Outside China, the spread of Covid-19 was worse in Italy, Iran, South Korea, and Japan. Not all of these countries have close proximity to China, yet lucrative prospects drew them in:

Italy, the most heavily affected country outside China as of March 10, was the first (and only) G-7 nation to sign onto the PRC's Belt and Road Initiative. In an attempt to prop up its weakening economy, Italy has also sought to capture the Chinese market for selling its luxury goods. With the outbreak now forcing Rome to put the country under lockdown, such prospects have been put on hold.

Italy also has signed scores of sister-city agreements with China, with the cities of Milan, Venice, and Bergamo included among them. These are the areas hardest-hit by the virus.

The Middle East Suffered

The Middle East, namely Iran, saw a surge in infections, specifically with government officials!

The Iranian regime has had a comprehensive strategic partnership with China since 2016, and its ties with Beijing began years before that. In violation of international sanctions, Iran has imported embargoed materials from China, while continuing to sell oil to the PRC. The Islamic Republic allowed flights in and out of four major Chinese cities until the end of February.

On-the-ground footage taken by Iranian citizens is reminiscent of the tragedy playing out in Wuhan, with overworked medical staff, despondent patients, and body bags lining hospital floors.

South Korea Suffered for its Ties to China

The South Korean people grew so tired of President Moon Jae-in for refusing to ban Chinese tourists they sent a massive signed petition that read:

Seeing Moon Jae-in's response to the new epidemic, we feel that he is more of a President for China than Korea.
                                        -- Petition Statement

Japan Suffered for its Ties to China

According to The Epoch Times, Japan, albeit not geo-strategically aligned with the PRC, placed profit over prudence. With millions of Chinese traveling to Japan for shopping and sightseeing annually, the country was slow to close its borders to mainland arrivals. Japan was among the first countries to report cases outside of China.

Recently, the CCP has attempted to portray its draconian handling of the coronavirus epidemic as a triumph for the Party's authoritarian system. But the Chinese historical record is more sobering. Throughout the centuries, plagues and other calamities signalled the downfall of imperial dynasties.

Today, the world is an interconnected community. Any country, community, or organization that keeps too close to the CCP and falls for its deception will taste the bitter fruits of that involvement.[1]

The CCP's Cultish Traits

According to the Nine Commentaries on the Communist Party, the CCP essentially fits the description of being a cult and although the Communist Party has never called itself a religion, it matches every single trait of a religion.

At the beginning of its establishment, it regarded Marxism as the absolute truth in the world. It piously **worshipped Marx as its spiritual God,** and exhorted people to engage in a life-long struggle for the goal of building a *"communist heaven on earth."*

The Communist Party does not believe in God and opposes traditional morality... It will do anything to keep in power with total disregard for morality, justice and human life... And today's CCP has become the largest ruling *"party of embezzlement and corruption"* in the world.

No Freedom of Conscience Allowed

The CCP is also afraid that the Chinese people might gain a sense of conscience and morality, so **it does not dare to allow the people to have faith in religion or freedom of thought.** It uses all its resources to persecute the good people who have faith, such as the underground Christians who believe in Jesus and God and the Falun Gong practitioners who seek to be, *"truthful, compassionate and tolerant."*

The CCP is afraid that democracy would end its one-party rule, so it does not dare to give people political freedom. **It acts swiftly to imprison independent liberals and civil rights activists.** It does, however, give people a deviated freedom. As long as you do not care about politics and do not oppose the CCP's leadership, you may let your desires go in any way you want, even if it means you do wicked, unethical things. As a result the CCP is deteriorating dramatically and social morality in China is experiencing an alarmingly sharp decline.[2]

So what about Taiwan
& Is Covid-19 Synthetic and Man-Made or Not?

No matter how China views Taiwan and how much of a nuisance or embarrassment to the CCP, Taiwan has emerged as a major player in the whole Covid-19's - big reveal to the world.

The origin of Covid-19 is of grave importance, and like you, I've heard every theory going, which are many! Still, nothing is adding up yet. Here, I have taken excerpts from an article where a professor in aetiology at the National Taiwan University claims, *(as many others have also already speculated)*, that the highly infectious virus could be synthetic *(man-made)*.

The Speculated Origin of the Respiratory Pathogen

The official conclusion by Chinese authorities is that a dingy wet market in Wuhan – Hubei's capital – was the source of the respiratory pathogen as animal-human transmission could have occurred there.

There has been much speculation about a virology institute in the city, affiliated with the Chinese Academy of Sciences, with rumours about a leakage due to slack management triggering a public health crisis worse than the SARS incident of 2003. Some of the more nonsensical talk includes a conspiracy theory that the United States "made" the virus to mass-infect Chinese people and stop the rise of its arch-rival.

Taiwan Scholar

Researchers likely synthesized the Covid-19, although more studies are needed to be certain.
-- Professor Fang Chi-tai

According to Frank Chen *(Asia Times)*, during his presentation, Fang outlined several hypotheses raised by Taiwanese and overseas researchers, including the probability that the virus was *"man-made"* and was leaked from the Wuhan Institute of Virology due to gross mismanagement.

Fang said the Wuhan facility's biosafety level-4 laboratory was used to store, handle and research samples of SARS, Ebola and other deadly infectious viruses.

Given China's poor track record of lab safety management, including a leakage of the SARS virus at a state lab in 2004, it is possible that a virus escaped from the Wuhan facility and resulted in the epidemic.

-- Professor Fang Chi-tai

Now, I'll interject here again, to say I've heard all the breathless theories, especially about bats, which quickly get debunked *(at least officially)*. And I'm sure, that we've all lost any original enthusiasm at this point. Lost interest is mainly due to the fact that we all just want to get back to work and get on with our normal lives. "Breaking news" - fades into background noise at this juncture.

Nonetheless, professor Fang Chi-tai persistently claimed that *"analyses of the Covid-19 virus have shown that it had a 96% genetic similarity with an RaTG13 bat virus also stored at the institute, and that the Covid-19 could be 'manufactured' by modifying the RaTG13 virus."*

He also revealed that French researchers had discovered four more amino acids in the gene sequence of Covid-19 than other known coronaviruses, which could be added artificially to make the viral transmission easier. Fang's theory is that natural mutations of viruses will only result in small, singular changes, and it is suspicious to see a naturally mutated virus suddenly take on four amino acids.

Determining the source of the virus would have important implications for epidemiology, he added, saying that if the virus was indeed synthetic, then it could be easier for it to be eradicated.

Taiwan's Centre for Disease Control & Synthesizing Remdesivir

Meanwhile, Frank Chen of Asia Times continues by saying that Taiwan's top research institute Academia Sinica said its researchers had already developed an antibody testing method for Covid-19 infection and made encouraging progress in synthesizing remdesivir, a medicine that many believe could cure the infection.

Taiwan's Center for Disease Control sent serum samples from three people who had contact with Taiwan's first Covid-19 fatality to the Academia Sinica, as part of a joint effort to determine the source of that infection and if the three had developed antibodies. The initial tests showed that only one sample had antibodies for Covid-19 and SARS.

The sample was obtained from a Taiwanese business-person who was not listed as a confirmed case, as researchers believed his immune system had beaten the virus. Yet the institute said it was still a mystery whether a person who had recovered from a novel coronavirus infection could contract it again.

Another team at Taiwan's Institute of Chemistry has also succeeded in synthesizing 100mg of remdesivir.

The synthesized drug cannot be used without the consent of a U.S. pharmaceutical firm that manufactures remdesivir. It was reported that Taiwan was negotiating a technology transfer deal to start mass production of the antiviral drug.

Discovery of its Origin

Remdesivir is a novel drug developed by the California-based Gilead Sciences as a treatment for Ebola virus and Marburg virus infections, and it has subsequently been found to show antiviral activity against other viruses.

Based on its success against other coronavirus infections, Gilead provided remdesivir to physicians that treated an American patient infected with Covid-19 and was offering the compound to China for a pair of trials in infected individuals with and without severe symptoms.

The mystery of how and where the virus started may take longer to discover than the cure.[3]

Lessons Learned from Taiwan

In time we will hear of all the developments, meanwhile Taiwan remains a political thorn in China's side, a cause of embarrassment, and exposure. Despite its proximity to, and extensive business with, mainland China, Taiwan has seen a relatively small number of infections. On January 26, Johns Hopkins University identified Taiwan as having the second-highest risk of epidemic spread outside China. However, robust prevention measures have proven effective.

Sources from the Epoch Times say that Taiwan officials began to board planes and assess passengers on December 31, 2019, after Wuhan authorities first confirmed the outbreak. In early February, Taiwan banned entry to foreign nationals who had travelled to the PRC. As of March 10, there were just 47 confirmed cases in Taiwan. The self-ruled island has been held as a model for epidemic control, *(despite being repeatedly denied participation in the CCP-friendly WHO).*

As China affairs commentator Heng He put it, Taiwan has a clear understanding of the communist regime and may be the only state that learned the lessons of the 2003 SARS outbreak, which also began in China. In Hong Kong, which has seen millions of residents stand up to Beijing's encroachment on the city's freedoms and rule of law since last year, the outbreak has been similarly subdued.[4]

❖

CHAPTER 8

The Major Plagues
(Of Recent Times)

Covid-19 – The Facts,
The Changing Alias of The CCP Virus

The novel Coronavirus or Covid-19 began life as "The Chinese Virus." Reason: it came from China, like the deadly Spanish Flu came from Spain!

Experts in the field of infectious-diseases will substantiate that discovering where an outbreak originates, is of paramount importance in procuring a cure, such as vaccine. Once again, I quote Tucker Carlson who said,

China is the largest country in the world. When the Chinese distort critical datasets - like how many

*people are infected or how many are dying - that
directly affects how every other country in the
world responds to the disease. We may have wasted
months assuming things about the coronavirus that
were not true. There's a big cost to that.* But more
broadly, we should be worried about what comes after this.
-- *Tucker Carlson*[1]

Distorting Global Dialogue

It is widely documented at this point that China withheld
and even censored information that was absolutely pertinent
and crucial towards lifesaving investigations. Instead
China gave misleading data to distort the global dialogue.
The original information circulating was false, especially
downplaying how *contagious* Covid-19 was.

Correct and timely information would have saved
countless lives and allowed for proper preparation to take
place. Instead, countries were blindsided and China's
irresponsible *control-of-the-information-flow* cost the world
community valuable time. It is unthinkable, the position that
China took to hinder the process and then blame-shift - from
culprit to victim - with deliberate and masterful propaganda.

The result of all this is that countries immediately
began turning on one another with bitter pointed-fingers of
accusation. *(China and other enemies of the West could now fold
their arms with glee).* What strategy! The West is sick, eaten by
a virus and politically self-destructs. *The EU is imploding!*
And just the very refusal to shut down its own wet-markets
is monumentally and unquestionably irresponsible.

Basic Medical Definitions

H1N1 (aka Swine Flu): **1:** a virus that is a subtype (H1N1) of the orthomyxovirus (species *Influenza A virus* of the genus *Influenzavirus A*) causing influenza A, that infects birds, pigs, and humans, and that includes strains which may occur in seasonal epidemics or sometimes pandemics ... by the third week of April it was established that the illness resulted from a triple recombination of human, avian, and swine influenza viruses; the virus has been found to be *H1N1.* — Lindsey R. Baden et al., *The New England Journal of Medicine,* 18 June 2009. Last year, older people had some immunity to the *H1N1* virus because it resembled strains that circulated decades ago. — Blythe Bernhard, *The St. Louis Post-Dispatch,* 16 January 2011.

NOTE: The subtype H1N1 is distinguished by a mutation of hemagglutinin (H1) that affects the ability of the virus to infect cells, and a mutation of a neuraminidase (N1) that enables the release of the replicated virus from cells.

2: influenza caused by the H1N1 virus *especially:* SWINE FLU. If you or your child came down with influenza during the *H1N1,* or swine flu, outbreak in 2009, it may not have happened the way you thought it did. — Nicholas Bakalar, *The New York Times,* 3 February 2011.

Thankfully, the *H1N1* flu didn't turn into the doomsday bug that some scientists feared. — *The Chicago Tribune,* 17 April 2010.[2]

SARS: A severe respiratory illness that is caused by a coronavirus (species *Severe acute respiratory syndrome-related virus* of the genus *Betacoronavirus*), is transmitted especially by contact with infectious material (such as respiratory droplets or body fluids), and is characterized by fever, headache, body aches, a dry cough, hypoxia, and usually pneumonia.

— called also *severe acute respiratory syndrome*
— see SARS-COV

First Known Use of SARS
2003, in the meaning defined above
History and Etymology for SARS
Severe acute respiratory syndrome[3]

MERS: A serious viral respiratory illness that is marked by fever, cough, and shortness of breath and that may often progress to severe pneumonia with acute respiratory distress syndrome and organ failure.

Note: MERS is caused by a coronavirus (species *Middle East respiratory syndrome-related coronavirus* of the genus *Betacoronavirus*) related to the causative virus of SARS. The first cases of MERS appeared in Saudi Arabia and most cases originate from countries in or near the Arabian Peninsula.

— see MERS-COV

First Known Use of MERS
2013, in the meaning defined above
History and Etymology for MERS
Middle East respiratory syndrome[4]

❖

CHAPTER 9

The Predicted Death of a Leader

The Abolishment of the UN
- Prophesied by Kim Clement

The next two chapters are very important to the body of Christ as there is a battle going on between the antichrist and us! The Church is having a woke moment.

I want to point to the late Kim Clement, who prophesied several times about the death of Kim Jong-un and how God will move supernaturally through a united Korea. He spoke of the shaking of nations many times. Here are just a few excerpts:

God said a sign shall be this - two signs shall I give you: one shall be the death of a leader who shall rapidly deteriorate in Korea. For God said, I will take both North and South and make it one. Kim, your days are numbered, says the Lord… I'm speaking of the Prime Minister of North Korea. God said enough is enough.

-- *Kim Clement*
15.9.2006

South Korea, North Korea shall become one, says the Lord. North Korea, your President is dead, he is already dead, I have already written on the wall, "mene, mene, tekel, parsin." God said, your days are numbered, you have been counted in the balance… Therefore, Kim, it is now time for you to face… this that you have done has been iniquitous. You are no longer alive, you are a vegetable, you are brain dead. And God said… I will cause that to bring about unity… in South and North Korea and the greatest move of the Spirit shall come from there.

-- *Kim Clement*
4.4.2009

And the little leader Kim Jong-un in North Korea is in trouble and has itchy fingers. His hands are trembling. It seems to me that everything will explode.

-- *Kim Clement*
29.9.2014

I shall not allow the corruption that has been in North Korea to continue. I have told the earth, there shall be a united Korea. I have told the earth that I will bring the greatest revival in North Korea, South Korea.

-- *Kim Clement*
31.12.2014

Do not be afraid of North Korea, do not be afraid of Iran; do not be afraid of the nations, for in 2016 everything will change says the Lord. There will be a sound of liberty from the White House, There will be a sound of prayers from the White House.

-- *Kim Clement*
29.8.2015[1]

Biblical Reference

*"Yet now be strong, Zerubbabel," says the Lord; "and be strong, Joshua, son of Jehozadak, the high priest; and be strong, all you people of the land," says the Lord, "and work; for I am with you," says the Lord of hosts. "According to the word that I covenanted with you when you came out of Egypt, so **My Spirit remains among you; do not fear!"***

*"For thus says the Lord of hosts: 'Once more (it is a little while) I will shake heaven and earth, the sea and dry land; **AND I WILL SHAKE ALL THE NATIONS...** '"*
(Haggai 2:4-8 NKJV)

Kim's prophecy back in 2009 about North Korea's leader: ***"You are no longer alive, you are a vegetable, you are brain dead."*** What's interesting about this is that during the writing of this particular book, reports of Kim's passing were all over the news. Did he get Covid-19? We won't know, the hermit nation is paranoid and that information will never be made known, nonetheless North Korea's Leader went invisible for a significant period, leaving everyone guessing and speculating.

Autocratic Power Structures MUST BE BROKEN

However, these are the regimes that have killed many Christians, pastors and missionaries. We must never believe that God is indifferent to this, for He will avenge their unjust slaughter. BUT there are set times for these things to take place and biblical predictions must take place in their rightful hour. In the meantime we must never imagine that God is ignorant.

The bible has been written along covenant lines, then ratified and sealed in the very blood of the Lamb, which is unbreakable.

Does Judgement have a Role Even in The New Testament?

Some people of a more delicate disposition will ask, "Well I don't believe God would kill North Korea's Leader like that! He wouldn't strike him that way, would He?" Well, to be biblically illiterate, is not advised. To understand the role of judgment, even in the New Testament, all we need do is pick up our bibles.

Despotic Herod was Struck the Death-Blow & Eaten by Worms!

After Herod had a thorough search made for him and did not find him [Peter], he cross-examined the guards and ordered that they be executed. Then Herod went from Judea to Caesarea and stayed there. He had been quarreling with the people of Tyre and Sidon; they now joined together and sought an audience with him.

After securing the support of Blastus, a trusted personal servant of the king, **they asked for peace, because they depended on the king's country for their food supply.**

On the appointed day Herod, wearing his royal robes, sat on his throne and delivered a public address to the people. They shouted, "This is the voice of a god, not of a man." **Immediately, because Herod did not give praise to God, an angel of the Lord struck him down, and he was eaten by worms and died.** *But the word of God continued to spread and flourish.*

(Acts 12:19-25)

Firstly, notice how it says, *"they depended on the king's country for their food supply."* Totalitarian, socialist communist governments with that autocratic spirit, always cause their people to be *"dependent"* upon the State, rather than helping them towards *"independence"* and self-rule. To control the food supply *(amongst other basic necessities),* and keeping people on food stamps for example, admits governments much more control.

The Vast Difference between "Equality" and "Liberty"

Democratically elected governments, on the other hand, which have been elected *"by the people/for the people"* are more inclined towards independence and freedom. There is a huge difference between *"equality"* and *"liberty."* In basic terms: **Equality at all costs is communism** *(no class and no private property).* **Liberty at all costs is democracy.** They both have very different ends and use very different means.

One party rule such as China's CCP, is reliant on total compliance and complete population control, with zero toleration for dissent or rebellion. In contrast, here in Italy, there are *"too many"* political parties, which put politics in a permanent state of *"stalemate"* and *"deadlock"* and to languish in an *"inefficient quagmire"* *(but we will get to that later).*

Which then is worse - an authoritarian structure that can get things done and fix long-term goals, like China or the inefficient, noisy and unpredictability of the democracies of the West? Well, one kills its opposition and has little to do with human rights or civil liberties and the other protects them. *(I think this answers the question!)*

Biblical Illiteracy vs.
Divinely Predicted & Set "Times"

To be on the same page as God and what He is doing in the earth, we must be biblically literate. To *"misunderstand"* God's agenda however, means that we will end up fighting Him and getting in His way. There are set times for everything. Daniel said that the antichrist will try to *"change the times,"* which is precisely why we the Church must understand those set *"times"* and *"purposes"* as God reveals them. This will allow us to unite in strength and to pray that God's will be done in the earth TODAY:

> *He will speak against the Most High and oppress his holy people and* **try to change the set times and the laws.** *The holy people will be delivered into his hands for a time, times and half a time.*
>
> *(Daniel 7:25)*

Clearly, by this account the antichrist will also be found outside of his legal *jurisdiction* and therefore, eventually taken out. But not before he tries to totally DISRUPT the *"set times"* of God that MUST TAKE PLACE. And all the kingdoms of this world will be handed over to the people of God:

> But the court will sit, and his power will be taken away and completely destroyed forever. **Then the sovereignty, power and greatness of all the KINGDOMS under heaven will be handed over to the holy people of the Most High.** His kingdom will be an everlasting kingdom, and all rulers will worship and obey him.
>
> This is the end of the matter. I, Daniel, was deeply troubled by my thoughts, and my face turned pale, but I kept the matter to myself.
>
> (Daniel 7:26-28)

Herod represented a totalitarian, autocratic, authoritarian government system of rule and acted every inch like a despotic ruler. He had put Peter in prison, but an angel did a jailbreak number on him! Herod had already killed James and now he wanted to make a spectacle of killing Peter. BUT the angel of the Lord struck him.

The same angel of the Lord is still in possession of his powers today! This is still the New Testament we are living in, Amen.

❖

CHAPTER 10

All Authority

Jurisdiction & Structure

Notice, in the entire world, its systems and structures of authority can only operate within its jurisdiction; outside of that, they are powerless and can be taken out. *(If it didn't matter, then it wouldn't be mentioned in the bible!)*

Ephesian 6:12 is another good example of hierarchy and the need for structure for authority to operate. This is why government exists, both spiritually and naturally. *("Of the increase of his GOVERNMENT... there shall be no end..." Isaiah 9:7 KJV)*

SO, Herod clearly stepped out of his jurisdiction:

They shouted, "This is the voice of a god, not of a man." **Immediately, because Herod did not give praise to God, an angel of the Lord struck him down, and he was eaten by worms and died.** *But the word of God continued to spread and flourish.*

(Acts 12:22-24)

Even angels have their jurisdiction:

In the same way, there were heavenly messengers in rebellion **who went outside their rightful domain of authority and abandoned their appointed realms.** *God bound them in everlasting chains and is keeping them in the dark abyss of the netherworld until the judgment of the great day.*

(Jude 6 TPT)

Messengers also, **those who did not keep their own principality,** *but did leave their proper dwelling, to a judgment of a great day, in bonds everlasting, under darkness He hath kept,*

...because **they failed to keep their rightful positions and abandoned their appointed realms.**

(Jude 6 VOICE)

Likewise, as the powerful victorious Church of Almighty God, we must know our jurisdiction and stay within it. We are untouchable: *"I tell you that you are Peter and on this rock I will build my church, and the gates of Hades will not overcome it" (Matthew 16:18).* "Gates" represent ruling structures, with proper jurisdiction. Herod was after Peter; but clearly had no jurisdiction.

The Sleeping Giant vs. Social Justice Warriors

The fact of the matter is this, if the Church doesn't arise out of its slumber and heavy-lidded stupor, events like this pandemic *(Covid-19)* will reoccur, where millions of jobs EVAPORATE in a short space of time.

There is a shifting going on and the Church needs to be a vehicle for REFORMATION, not for its usual lethargy or irrelevant hyperactivity. It needs to get into politics *(local and national)*, even if it doesn't want to. It's mandated by the Lord, that the corridors of power in world affairs, aught to be influenced by the CHURCH, not a sleeping, useless, self-centred, procrastinating and narcissistic giant!

As busy as we should be reforming institutions for the glory of the Lord, China and other bad actors are subverting them, from the ground up; like reformation in reverse, that looks to "dismantle" and undermine them, rather than reform them. BUT we'll discuss how our institutions and our education systems have all been hijacked and subverted to the point they're becoming unrecognisable.

Churches, especially Evangelical Christian and Conservative charitable organisations are told not to proselytise the refugees they feed, as it risks *"offending"* them. The very point of such organisations is to feed the spirit, soul and body of the needy. Without which, the Church again is irrelevant. Big donors bribe and mute many institutions and organisations, which we have held sacred for generations and none more sacred than the Church. *(WHAT! Is this giant mute as well as sleeping?)*

Plus we now have activist preachers, teachers and pastors who've become trendy social-justice-warriors, who preach social justice sermons, without using any biblical references. And our college classrooms and university auditoriums have become sect-like and cultish in their agenda, where Marxist educators deliberately indoctrinate our youngest and brightest in order to infiltrate the next generation. This has been a sly-grassroots and long-term strategy.

We Won't Recognise Tomorrow
If we don't Arise TODAY!

HOW? Technology won't bring about reformation. World rulers won't bring about reformation. ONLY GOD CAN BRING ABOUT REFORMATION TO THE NATIONS THROUGH HIS RULING STRUCTURE - THE CHURCH.

Trump, for example, is believed to be a modern version of the biblical Cyrus, but while he holds office today, there's no guarantee for tomorrow *(no guarantee that he'll get in for a second term)*. It is what it is, and we must not misplace our trust for God by placing it in a man, no matter how divinely placed he may be -*"for such a time as this."* (God will not share His glory with anyone, as Herod learned!)

The "Kingdom" Suffers Violence

This is the truth: no one who has ever been born to a woman is greater than John the Baptist. And yet the most insignificant person in the kingdom of heaven is greater than he. All of the prophets of old, all of the law — that was all prophecy leading up to the coming of John.

Now, that sort of prepares us for this very point, right here and now. **When John the Baptist came, <u>the kingdom of heaven</u> began to break in upon us, and those in power are trying to clamp down on it—why do you think John is in jail?**

If only you could see it — John is the Elijah, the prophet we were promised would come and prepare the way. He who has ears for the truth, let him hear.

(Matthew 11:11-15 VOICE)

ANY ACHIEVEMENTS made by the Trump Administration *(along with every other conservative, freedom loving government across the globe)*, will be washed away for good, if we rest on our morals and don't rise up to TAKE the hour that God has given us.

"BY POLITICAL FORCE?" "NO!" "BY CHURCH FORCE!" By the body of Christ coming together as a galvanized covenant force - in powerful unity - with a full comprehension and revelation of Her place in God's ruling structure. Filling her position with authority and not allowing the devil to fill the vacuum. We must not surrender that power.

Empty Power Vacuums Don't Stay Empty Long!

*When an impure spirit comes out of a person, it goes through arid places seeking rest and does not find it. Then it says, "I will return to the house I left." **When it arrives, it finds the house UNOCCUPIED, swept clean and put in order.** Then it goes and takes with it* *seven other spirits more wicked than itself, and they go in and live there. And the final condition of that person is worse than the first. That is how it will be with this wicked generation.*

(Matthew 12:43-45)

Space must be occupied and if we don't possess it the devil will. The devil will find what's *"empty and put in order"* and will fill it to the brim with wickedness and evil intent and purposes. We must fully occupy what God has given us. Whatever genre it is, whether it's the arts, entertainment, business, politics, and education and so forth, if the Church is not filling the void, the devil will. *(We need to take back our education system for instance, before Marxist socialists re-write our history books!)*

The World Health Organisation recently joined forces with Lady Gaga and other artists for the *"One World: Together at Home"* venture. Enough said!

CHURCH OF GOD COME ALIVE! STOP WITH ALL YOUR INTROSPECTION & SELF-ABSORBED-BROODING! GET IN YOUR DESIGNATED LANE & POSSESS IT. YOU'RE NOT A VESTIGE OF A BYGONE ERA WHEN CHURCH MATTERED. YOU MATTER NOW!

This is the Time of Kingdoms and Nations

We must have a "KINGDOMS" and "NATIONS" mentality, because God has and we are His people. There can be no, business as usual attitude. This is a geopolitical era, and we are plum in it. There's no getting out of it. Here we are. It is the battle of nations and God is still speaking right into it today.

God's not merely dealing with individuals, *(coddling and pampering their selfish needs)*. He's not merely catering to random individual agendas, but to His own. Scripture declares that we are called according to His purpose (Romans 8:28). As KING OF KINGS, this signifies there is more than one kingdom but Christ's is the preeminent.

As the Church of the living God, we are to make His presence felt in the earth. Our prayers are not empty rhetoric, religious sounding chatter or ritualistic noise. We are not conjuring our words into vain babblings or charismatic witchcraft *(2 Timothy 2:16)*.

How to Pray Against these Ruling Structures

Right now the devil has more authority than the church in world affairs. Why? - Because the Church left a vacuum and the devil took it. How then should we be praying, at a time like this? Pray for the antichrist autocratic ruling structures *(that are attempting to "force events" in order to "change the times" – just as Daniel's prophecy warned)* be broken down. Pray that they be *shattered and scattered*, in Jesus' mighty name. *(See Genesis chapter 11, God's response to the tower of Babel was to "scatter" them)*.

This is the time when the antichrist is looking to take his place. The Church of almighty God must remember what it is and that the gates *(ruling structures)* of hell will not prevail against it. We must not allow this spirit of the antichrist, with its spirit of autocracy to take over and allow its false prophet *(the fake news media)* to tell us what we are.

Communism Broken & a United Korea!

God's prophet, declared a united Korea and that a powerful move of God will flow out of it. The last thing the antichrist wants is a united Korea. The last thing China wants is a united Korea. That would represent a ruling structure with its own jurisdiction – with power to oppose it's anti-God agenda.

It doesn't want a democratic challenger right on its doorstep, with powerful jurisdiction. Korea has been a tool of leverage for China for a long time, especially in its trade war with the U.S. government. Korea will be a hub of revival yet again, as it was before, *(it had a powerful connection to the Azusa Street Revival in 1906, until communism took over at the end of WWII)*.

Once again, the Church must rise up and pray for these AUTOCRATIC RULING STRUCTURES OF COMMUNISM to be broken apart and its yoke of bondage to be removed from the neck of every nation that it has subdued.

> *Either communism must die or Christianity must die, because it's actually a battle between Christ and Anti-Christ.*
>
> *-- Billy Graham 1954*

A Great Awakening

Church, this period is a wake up call. The world uses the term *"woke"* to describe this. The church must be *"woke,"* but not to the propaganda and deception of this world, but to the truth of what God wants to do in the earth today. Listen, we know who we are, the Church is a veritable force to be reckoned with, a divine *"ruling structure"* positioned in the earth for the purposes of almighty God, a force that cannot be prevailed against.

Amen. Come, Lord Jesus.

(Revelation 22:20)

To continue, please read book 3, "Watchers of the Four Kings," China, Russia, America and the UK plus Arab Islamic Nations – all jostling for World Domination.

❖

Endnotes

Chapter 1 China's Ambitions & Cover Up

1. https://www.longlongtimeago.com/once-upon-a-time/myths/myths-from-china/one-sun-in-the-sky/

2. https://www.foxnews.com/opinion/tucker-carlson-who-lap dog-china-coronavirus

3. https://en.wikipedia.org/wiki/World_Health_Organization

Chapter 2 The Silver Lining

1. https://subsplash.com/houseofdestiny/media/mi/+r3c2xmp

2. Jianli Yang April 17, 2020 2:55 PM; https://www.nationalreview.com/2020/04/who-chief-tedros-has-got-to-go/

   https://www.nationalreview.com/2020/04/who-chief-tedros-has-got-to-go/?jwsource=cl

   Some excerpts taken, information, paraphrased and adapted from article "WHO Chief Tedros has got to Go"

   Jianli Yang is the founder and president of Citizen Power Initiatives for China. Aaron Rhodes is the president of the Forum for Religious Freedom-Europe, the human-rights editor of Dissident magazine, and the author of The Debasement of Human Rights.

3. https://www.npr.org/sections/goatsandsoda/2020/04/15/835011346/a-timeline-of-coronavirus-comments-from-president-trump-and-who

4. https://en.wikipedia.org/wiki/United_States_withdrawal_from_the_United_Nations; Paraphrased

Chapter 4 It's all about the "Science"

1. https://www.foxnews.com/politics/coronavirus-stay-at-home-orders-protests-economy?fbclid=IwAR2R0zqyXhHh9sBZUu1ipr D4gKdFGWu2G8JNW9XC8GBLvFPlZoE8HjWgElY

2. https://www.theepochtimes.com/sunlight-heat-and-humidity-are-detrimental-to-ccp-virus-dhs-official_3324940.html?v=ul

Chapter 5 A Different Battle Field

1. http://www.xinhuanet.com/english/2019-08/27/c_138340586.htm

2. https://www.thelocal.it/20200417/coronavirus-italian-government-reveals-plans-to-use-tracking-app

3. https://www.thepatent.news/2020/04/17/coronavirus-tracking-app-immuni/; Alessio Iannicelli, 17 April 2020 in Mobile Tech

4. By Adam Satariano, March 10, 2019; https://www.nytimes.com/interactive/2019/03/10/technology/internet-cables-oceans.html

Chapter 6 Britain's China Policy

1. https://www.telegraph.co.uk/news/2020/05/04/us-spy-planes-could-pulled-britain-white-house-conducts-major/

https://www.organiser.org/Encyc/2020/4/6/Britain-pulls-out-of-5G-contract-with-Huawei.html

Ben Riley-Smith, U.S. Editor, 4 May 2020; only some excerpts used - in part – very paraphrased

2. https://www.newsweek.com/huawei-boris-johnson-conservative-rebellion-churchill-farage-1488582; Nigel Farage is senior editor-at-large of Newsweek's "The Debate" platform, 22/02/20; excerpts paraphrased

3. https://www.theepochtimes.com/perspective-on-the-pandemic-british-pms-ties-with-the-chinese-regime_3316330.html?v=ul; April 17, 2020, Updated: April 19, 2020; Tian Yun

Chapter 7 Chinese Communist Ties Suffer Most from Covid-19

1. The Epoch Times Editorial Board; https://www.theepochtimes.com/where-ties-with-communist-china-are-close-the-corona virus-follows_3268389.html; March 11, 2020, Updated: April 27, 2020; excerpts taken and paraphrased

2. http://www.ninecommentaries.com/english-8

3. By Frank Chen February 25, 2020; https://asiatimes.com/2020/02/covid-19-may-be-man-made-claims-taiwan-scholar/; paraphrased excerpts

4. https://www.theepochtimes.com/where-ties-with-communist-china-are-close-the-coronavirus-follows_3268389.html

Chapter 8 The Major Plagues (Of Recent Times)

1. https://www.foxnews.com/opinion/tucker-carlson-propagan da-war-china-coronavirus

2. "H1N1" Merriam-Webster.com Medical Dictionary, Merriam-Webster, https://www.merriam-webster.com/medical/H1N1. Accessed 6 Apr. 2020

3. "SARS" Merriam-Webster.com Dictionary, Merriam-Webster, https://www.merriam-webster.com/dictionary/SARS. Accessed 6 Apr. 2020

4. "MERS" Merriam-Webster.com Dictionary, Merriam-Webster, https://www.merriam-webster.com/dictionary/MERS. Accessed 6 Apr. 2020

   List of outbreaks from China since 2000 – list is too extensive – can be found in foot notes https://www.who.int/csr/don/archive/country/chn/en/

Chapter 9 The Predicted Death of a Leader

1. https://www.bitchute.com/channel/lancewallnau/;
   https://www.bitchute.com/video/vuV1WGFtoaIF/;
   https://www.lancewallnau.com;
   https://www.7mu.com;
   https://www.facebook.com/lancewallnau

Bible translations

- Unless otherwise indicated, all scriptural quotations are from the HOLY BIBLE, NEW INTERNATIONAL VERSION ®. NIV ®. Copyright © 1973, 1978, 1984 by the International Bible Society. Used by permission of Zondervan Publishing House. All rights reserved.

- Scripture quotations marked AMP are taken from the Amplified® Bible, Copyright © 2015 by The Lockman Foundation. Used by permission. (www.Lockman.org)

- Scripture quotations marked NKJV are taken from the New King James Version®. Copyright © 1982 by Thomas Nelson, Inc. Used by permission. All rights reserved.

- Scripture quotations marked TPT are from The Passion Translation®. Copyright © 2017, 2018 by Passion & Fire Ministries, Inc. Used by permission. All rights reserved. ThePassionTranslation.com

- Scripture quotations marked VOICE are taken from The Voice™. Copyright © 2008 by Ecclesia Bible Society. Used by permission. All rights reserved.

❖

Ministry Profile

Doctor Alan Pateman, an apostle, is the President and Founder of **"Alan Pateman Ministries International"** (APMI), which was established in England back in 1987, a Christian-based *(parachurch)* non-profit and non-denominational outreach. This ministry is now focusing in two main areas: First **"Connecting for Excellence"** Apostolic Networking (CFE) and secondly, the teaching arm, **"LifeStyle International Christian University"** (LICU).

CFE is a multi-facetted missions organisation with the purpose of connecting leaders for divine opportunities and building lasting relationships, to touch the lives of leaders literally the world over. Apostle Dr Alan Pateman has to date ordained more than 500 ministers in over 50 NATIONS. In addition there are ministries, churches and schools who are in Association or Affiliation, looking to him for apostolic counsel and oversight.

Secondly LICU, which was founded in 2007, is a study program to help people discover their purpose and destiny. A global network of university campuses and correspondence students, demonstrating the Supernatural Kingdom of God through Doctrinal, Apostolic and Prophetic Teaching. Dr Alan holds the position of President/CEO, Professor of Theology, Biblical Studies and Apostolic Ministry. LICU is exploding throughout Europe, Asia and Africa, enhancing the Body of Christ.

Dr Alan has authored more than 40 books including numerous teaching materials and LICU university courses (30) along with hundreds of Truth for the Journey articles on kingdom lifestyle *(that are regularly distributed globally via the internet).*

He is recognised as an Apostle, Bishop, Leadership Mentor, University Educator, Motivational Speaker, Connector and Author, who has also been featured on national and international TV and radio networks throughout the years.

Currently Apostle Alan, his wife Dr Jennifer reside in Lucca *(Tuscany)* Italy and travel out from their Apostolic Company.

- Alan Pateman Ph.D., D.Min., D.D., M.A., B.Th.

Academic Background

Dr. Alan Pateman attended several colleges throughout his training *(including studying Theology at Roffey Place, Horsham, UK and a Member of Kerygma - with Rev. Colin Urquhart and Dr. Bob Gordon - 1985-1987)* before being awarded a Doctorate of Divinity *(2006)* in recognition of his lifetime achievements by the International College of Excellence, now "DanEl Christian College" *(President: Dr. Robb Thompson USA)* also "Life Christian University" *(Dr. Douglas Wingate USA)* where he also earned a Bachelor of Theology B.Th. *(2006),* a Master of Arts in Theology M.A., a Doctor of Ministry in Theology D.Min., *(2007)* and Doctor of Philosophy in Theology Ph.D. *(2013)* from LICU.

❖

To Contact the Author

Please email:

Alan Pateman Ministries International

Email: apostledr@alanpateman.com
Web: www.AlanPatemanMinistries.com

*Please include your prayer requests
and comments when you write.*

❖

Other Books

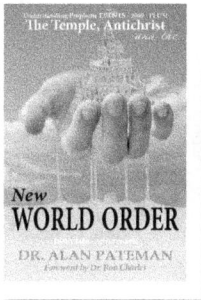

The Temple, Antichrist and the New World Order (End Times - Series Three)

The lives of everyone will be profoundly affected, even destroyed, culminating in the Battle of Armageddon. Many say that now is the time, it is this generation, that has been called to live out our destiny during the period that the ancients called the "birth pangs of the Messiah."

ISBN: 978-1-909132-73-3, Pages: 168, Format: Paperback, Published: 2018
Also available in eBook format!

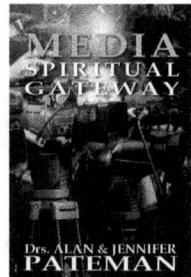

Media, Spiritual Gateway

Let's face it; we live in the era of fake news! It's always existed, but never been quite so prominent. Today it's an all-out-war between fact and political fiction. The media has been sabotaged by political activism. Gone are the days of impartiality and objective unbiased reporting, with many sources saying that true journalism is dead.

ISBN: 978-1-909132-54-2, Pages: 192, Format: Paperback, Published: 2018
Also available in eBook format!

Truth for the Journey Books

Forgiveness, The Key to Revival

Scripture is absolute when it comes to forgiveness. IF we forgive, THEN we are forgiven. It's that simple but no one said it was easy! Nonetheless, forgiveness can be likened to a spiritual key that unlocks spiritual doors and opportunities!

ISBN: 978-1-909132-41-2, Pages: 124, Format: Paperback, Published: 2013
Also available in eBook format!

Healing and Deliverance, A Present Reality

Within the pages of this book (which has to be a "must-read" for any serious enquirer into the Healing and Deliverance Ministry), Dr Alan unfolds a different pathway, so that the heartbeat of God's message of God's total deliverance can be released into the church of Jesus Christ today.

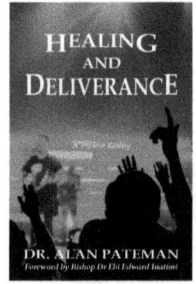

ISBN: 978-1-909132-80-1, Pages: 188, Format: Paperback, First Print: 1994
Also available in eBook format!

Empowered to Overcome

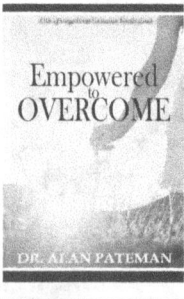

This book provides some hefty reinforcement for all believers; designed by Dr Pateman to bolster their faith by providing a refresher course for those who are more seasoned and lessons in sound fundaments for those who are new.

ISBN: 978-0-9570654-4-4, Pages: 100, Format: Paperback, Published: 2020
Also available in eBook format!

LIFESTYLE
UNIVERSITY

Raising Up
Christian Leaders

Dear Friends,

Have you considered becoming one of our international students? We are privileged to welcome you, from around the world, to "LifeStyle International Christian University" *(the teaching arm of Alan Pateman Ministries International).* **An English speaking university** dedicated to your success; to see you trained and equipped to fully succeed in your God given Destiny.

It is our passion to raise up the leaders of tomorrow, who will have influence in all realms of authority, including the Body of Christ. Men and women of strategy, wisdom and true godliness, who'll stand with stature and maturity in this hour.

It's undeniable that in today's world, recognised education has become indispensable, therefore it is our desire to offer well balanced and well structured courses. Those that have been written by gifted and talented ministers of God, who seek to be inspired by God's Holy Spirit.

Consequently we have put together a **flexible curriculum,** designed both for correspondence students and campuses, which is a strategy to reach the distant learner; whether provincial, national or international. In fact we have many correspondence students from around the world, including a growing number of successful campuses, in various countries.

This is a growing platform, where men and women of dignity and passion, can grow and be established in their God given endeavours. As God is the healer of the nations, we pray and believe that many of our alumni will go on to **become world changers** in their own right.

We are proud of each and every one of our LICU students.
It would be our pleasure if you would join them on this incredible journey!

Doctor Alan Pateman

Alan Pateman Prof. Ph.D., D.Min., D.D., M.A., B.Th.
PRESIDENT AND CEO
www.licuuniversity.com www.cfeapostolicnetwork.com
Email: info@licuuniversity.com Mob: +39 366 329 1315

For more information visit our website/facebook or contact our office, using the details below:

Website: www.licuuniversity.com
Facebook: www.facebook.com/LICUMainCampus
Email: info@licuuniversity.com
Telephone: +39 366 329 1315

ALAN PATEMAN MINISTRIES
PRESENTS

TEACHING - LEARNING - LIVING
A MASTER CLASS
with Dr Alan Pateman

DR. ALAN IS AVAILABLE TO HOLD TEACHING SEMINARS ON SATURDAYS WITH YOUR LEADERS / MEMBERS AND THEN MINISTER AT YOUR SUNDAY SERVICE. PLEASE CONTACT OUR OFFICE FOR AVAILABILITY.

CONTACT:
TEL. 0039 366 329 1315
APOSTLEDR@ALANPATEMAN.COM

www.alanpatemanministries.com

www.ingramcontent.com/pod-product-compliance
Lightning Source LLC
Chambersburg PA
CBHW050355280326
41933CB00010BA/1467